PIRATES of the CARIBBEAN

Bring Me That Horizon

THE MAKING OF

PIRATES of the CARIBBEAN

Written by Michael Singer

A WELCOME BOOK

EDITIONS

NEW YORK

For information address Disney Editions
114 Fifth Avenue, New York, NY 10011-5690.
Editorial Director: Wendy Lefkon
Senior Editor: Jody Revenson
Editorial Assistant: Jessica Ward

Produced by Welcome Enterprises, Inc.
6 West 18th Street, New York, NY 10011
www.welcomebooks.com
Project Director: H. Clark Wakabayashi

Designed by Timothy Shaner and Christopher Measom
nightanddaydesign.biz

Cover design by John Sabel, Steve Nuchols, and Ann Dooley

Photographs by Jerry Bruckheimer: pages 6–12; 68 (top);
90–91; 95; 148 (top).

Additional photographs in this book were taken by John Bramley,
Sam Emerson, Andrew Eccles, Greg Gorman, Nels Israelson,
Elliott Marks, Peter Mountain, and Stephen Vaughan

Page 25: *Marooned* (1909) by Howard Pyle (1853–1911). Oil on
canvas, 40 x 60 inches. Courtesy of the Delaware Art Museum.
Museum Purchase, 1912.

Pages 26–27: Collection of The New York Historical Society.
Courtesy of Bridgeman Art Library

Pages 28–29: *The Black Swan* © 1942 Twentieth Century Fox.
All rights reserved.

Page 41: Storyboards (second and third from top right)
by Anton Verbinski

Library of Congress Cataloging-in-Publication Data on file.

ISBN-13: 978-14231-0319-6   ISBN-10: 1-4231-0319-X

Printed in China
FIRST EDITION
10 9 8 7 6 5 4 3 2 1

DISNEYPIRATES.COM

THESE PAGES: Visual development
of Shipwreck City by Darek Gogol.

Pirates of the Caribbean: The Curse of the Black Pearl
Screen Story by Ted Elliott & Terry Rossio
and Stuart Beattie and Jay Wolpert
Screenplay by Ted Elliott & Terry Rossio

Pirates of the Caribbean: Dead Man's Chest
Pirates of the Caribbean: At World's End
Based on characters created by Ted Elliott & Terry Rossio
and Stuart Beattie and Jay Wolpert
Written by Ted Elliott & Terry Rossio

Based on Walt Disney's Pirates of the Caribbean
Produced by Jerry Bruckheimer
Directed by Gore Verbinski

Contents

Raising the Mainsail

PHOTO FOREWORD
Images by Jerry Bruckheimer

Whether drawn on the walls of prehistoric caves or painted in European studios or on canvas in an open field, people have always told stories in single, still images. With the creation and development of photography in the 1820s, a new and incalculably important form of creative expression was born. It was inevitable that someone would find a way to make these photographs move, and thanks to Lumiere, Edison, and other pioneers, they did, by the end of the same century. Perhaps it makes sense, then, that my love of the movies was preceded by a fascination with still photography. I love photography and I love taking pictures, which I've been doing since I was six years old. One of my favorite things about being a film producer is that it allows me to indulge my passion for photography on movie sets. And never, I think, have there been sets like the ones for the three Pirates of the Caribbean films.

From the great faces of the actors, whether the stars or the smallest bit players, to the amazingly picturesque Caribbean locations, to the massive sets and impressive ships, I couldn't resist taking my cameras in hand to try and capture some of the feeling of what it was like to be there when the cameras rolled on *The Curse of the Black Pearl, Dead Man's Chest,* and *At World's End.* There are so many interesting images that you can capture when you're on these fantasy movies. The director, Gore Verbinski, and cinematographer, Darek Wolski, are brilliant visualists, so when they set up such great shots they're doing me a big favor with the beautiful scenery, angles, and light. It was nice to be able to piggyback on them, and capture some of the wonderful images that they created. But I also like shooting my own behind-the-scenes material unrelated to the actual scenes, and in what follows, you'll see some examples of both approaches. I've put together a book of pictures that I have taken during production on all of the movies I've produced, and keep them as mementos. Here are a few images from what will go into my Pirates of the Caribbean book and I'd like to share them with you.

If it's true that one picture is worth a thousand words, then hopefully the photographs that follow will give you an immediate, visceral sense of the fabulous pirate world that we created. Hope you enjoy taking this peek behind the curtain. —Jerry Bruckheimer

OPPOSITE: I just *had* to photograph this stuntman in a very odd position on the Edinburgh Trader in St. Vincent's Wallilabou Bay.

ABOVE: Keira Knightley between shots in a thicket of dasheen plants in Hampstead, Dominica.

TOP: Orlando Bloom and Jack Davenport battle away during the three-way swordfight, despite the intense heat of the Dominican location.

ABOVE: Naomie Harris as Tia Dalma and the incredible design of her bayou shack were a perfect match.

OPPOSITE: Even Johnny Depp needs some quiet time on occasion, and he found it during a break in filming.

LEFT: Orlando Bloom and his beloved dog Sidi, rescued by the young actor while shooting on location in Morocco and brought back home to England; ABOVE: If still cameras existed in the 18th century, perhaps someone might have captured an image like this of a sailor in the rigging; BELOW LEFT: Pintel wearing shades? Lee Arenberg and Mackenzie Crook about to shoot, and of course, Lee will lose the sunglasses before the cameras roll.

BELOW: When you have a beautiful St. Vincent sunset like this, and costumed EITC soldiers in longboats, what else can you do but capture it on film? OPPOSITE TOP: The costume, hair, and makeup departments did amazing work on the Pelegostos. Here are two of the tribe's scarier members; OPPOSITE BOTTOM: Keira Knightley bursts into a laugh while getting drenched for her very serious opening scene of *Dead Man's Chest*.

Hitting the
High Seas

October 2005: Off the southeastern coast of Grand Bahama Island, the *Black Pearl*, having already gained film notoriety as the swiftest ship to sail the Seven Seas, bobs like a cork in a Jacuzzi with the whirlpool switched on "high." Although there's only a three-foot swell, hardly the worst that the company has seen in recent days, gusty winds blowing off a tropical depression 100 miles to the south have turned the Atlantic into an unstable, muddy force. Despite its sturdy build and heavy weight of 311 tons, the *Pearl* is pitching and rolling back and forth, a seesaw effect that plays havoc with any sense of equilibrium. On deck, not only maintaining their footing but also their retention of several lines of dialogue, Johnny Depp and Orlando Bloom act as if it's nothing out of the ordinary. Keira Knightley is curled up on some burlap sacks on the poop deck with literature that would not be described as a "beach read," awaiting her next scene. Producer Jerry Bruckheimer, whose Zenlike calm belies the fact that he runs one of the world's most successful film and television operations, is observing the filming—as well as carefully chronicling the moment on his own camera—as if the deck beneath his feet were rock steady. Director Gore Verbinski quietly gives directions to Depp and Bloom, director of photography Dariusz Wolski, and other behind-the-camera artists.

Strangely, the skies are mostly blue, with light, puffy clouds dotting the canopy. But there's something out there, and it's not to be taken lightly. Hurricanes Katrina and Rita have just taken a terrible toll in the states that border the Gulf of Mexico, and many of these storms have their roots within the warm waters of The Bahamas. A gust comes up, and the shrill whistle and howl blowing around the black sails of the *Pearl* create an ungodly wail. Verbinski rolls his ever-present (and usually unlit) cigar around in his mouth and keeps right on working, unperturbed.

For those of us who are more landlubbers than sea salts, the continuous rising and dropping of the horizon is an invitation to double over the rail and give back to the sea a little of what she gave to us.

Just another typical day on the set of Pirates of the Caribbean.

OPPOSITE: Captain Jack Sparrow's auspicious introduction in *The Curse of the Black Pearl*; ABOVE: Johnny Depp and Keira Knightley, knee-deep in the waters of Petit Tabac, St. Vincent.

In art, as in life, history has a strange way of coming full circle. The first on-screen image ever to appear in an all live-action feature by the Walt Disney Studios was none other than a close-up of the skull and crossbones Jolly Roger flag in the classic 1950 version of Robert Louis Stevenson's *Treasure Island*.

Some fifty-three years later, the very same studio spectacularly reinvigorated a moribund genre. Jerry Bruckheimer, Gore Verbinski, and a brilliant company of actors and behind-the-scenes artists breathed new life into tattered sails, inspired by the Disney theme park attraction that has enchanted generations since its 1967 debut at Disneyland in Anaheim. With clever references to the attraction's content sprinkled throughout, *Pirates of the Caribbean: The Curse of the Black Pearl* opened on July 9, 2003, and was a smash hit, amassing a worldwide box office total surpassing $653 million and defying some less than enthusiastic anticipation for a "movie based on a theme park attraction." The film received five Academy Award nominations, including Johnny Depp for Best Actor.

Like the attraction itself, *The Curse of the Black Pearl* appealed to that little bit of pirate that lives within us all—the desire for freedom, adventure, and not a small amount of mischief. While paying affectionate homage to the cinematic adventures that preceded it, *The Curse of the Black Pearl* sailed into entirely new territory, breaking with tradition by linking its high-seas tales with lashings of

ABOVE: Elizabeth Swann adorns herself with the Aztec gold pendant she's carefully kept since childhood; RIGHT: Jerry Bruckheimer on the battlements of Fort Charles; OPPOSITE TOP: Captain Jack and Barbossa battle in the treasure cave; OPPOSITE BOTTOM: Orlando Bloom on the *Lady Washington*.

Jerry Bruckheimer, Gore Verbinski, and a brilliant company of actor

...and behind-the-scenes artists breathed new life into tattered sails.

irreverent humor, as typified by Johnny Depp's startlingly inspired creation of Captain Jack Sparrow—a pirate the likes of which audiences had never seen before. From the moment of his initial mock-heroic entrance, standing tall on what turns out to be a sad little (and swiftly sinking) boat, millions of people instantly fell in love with this scurrilous buccaneer, who sashayed rather than swaggered, and gave off whiffs of impertinence, courage, cowardice, bad personal hygiene, a genius for self-preservation, and most profoundly, an adoration for his ship, the *Black Pearl*, and the seas it sailed upon.

While rooted in the fundamentals of classic Disney family films, *The Curse of the Black Pearl* proved that a "family film" could find a wholly contemporary groove, and spin with it until the wheels fell off. It also kicked off a groundswell of fascination for all things piratical, resulting in everything from a spate of new books about the seafaring scoundrels, to a boom in pirate-themed parties and dinner shows, not to mention "I ♥ Jack Sparrow" stickers plastered onto schoolgirls' binders all over the world.

Clearly, there was a mandate for more Pirates. Jerry Bruckheimer and Gore Verbinski, along with Walt Disney Pictures, decided that just one sequel would not be enough. It made practical and economical sense to film two follow-ups simultaneously, taking full advantage of locations, sets, and the availability of its increasingly in-demand stars. "We were hoping for the success of *The Curse of the Black Pearl* so that we could make more Pirates movies," notes Bruckheimer, "and after viewing the second and third films, you'll see that everything relates back to what started everything off in the first."

But not even Bruckheimer, Verbinski, nor the Walt Disney Studios could have predicted what would happen when *Pirates of the Caribbean: Dead Man's Chest,* opened on July 7, 2006. "Big Booty for Bruckaneers" screamed a headline of the Hollywood trade paper *Daily Variety.* On its opening three-day weekend, *Dead Man's Chest* amassed an astonishing $135.7 million, surpassing the previous champ, 2002's *Spider-Man,* by more than $20 million. Other United States box-office records were also toppled: the three-day numbers even beat the standing four-day weekend record; the Friday totals of $55.5 million set a new mark for the

ABOVE: Will plays Liar's Dice with Davy Jones; OPPOSITE: Captain Barbossa, Elizabeth, and Captain Jack Sparrow prepare to Parlay in *At World's End.*

biggest one-day numbers ever; and by Saturday, its $100.2 million take was the biggest ever two-day gross, which meant that *Dead Man's Chest* was the first movie in history to break the sacred $100 million mark in forty-eight hours. By the third weekend, the film soared past four major new releases and became the fastest film in history to pass the $300 million mark in the U.S. and Canada (breaking *The Curse of the Black Pearl's* $305 million milepost). It was the same story from Tokyo to Mumbai to Warsaw and back again. The legion of Pirates fans who lined up for hours swept across the demographic board, with some so comprehensively attired in an array of buccaneer gear that it looked as if they had stepped right off the set. By September 2006, *Dead Man's Chest* became only the third member of the billion dollar club—the third-highest grossing film, internationally, in motion picture history.

The massive, landmark triumph of *Dead Man's Chest* was certainly satisfying to Jerry Bruckheimer, Gore Verbinski, and the huge cast and crew who had left their friends and families for the very long voyage, much of it far away from home. But far from resting on their laurels, it was business-as-usual, with everyone working unabated to prepare for the remaining seventy days of filming for the third film, *At World's End.*

For despite the big-money business or the sirenlike promise of unimaginable acclaim, it all comes down to a collection of diverse and talented individuals—on both sides of the camera—trying the best they can to translate words on the written page into tangible images on the big screen. This is the story of one group of dreamers who defied the odds, tempted fate, rolled the dice, and came up very, very big winners.

A Pirate's Life for Them

We're rascals and scoundrels,
we're villians and knaves.

Drink up me 'earties, yo ho.

We're devils and black sheep
and really bad eggs.

Drink up me 'earties, yo ho.

Yo ho, yo ho, a pirate's life for me.

As long as there have been oceans, ships, and men and women to sail upon them, there have been other men and women seeking to take what they could—and give nothing back. Two thousand years before the likes of Edward "Blackbeard" Teach and "Calico Jack" Rackham were raising hell in the Caribbean, the ancient Mediterranean and Aegean trading routes were hotbeds of piracy. Romans had to contend with Saxon raiders from the Baltic. In the ninth century, the Vikings stormed out of the fjords of Norway and terrorized Northern Europe and the British Isles. Islamic sailors, known as corsairs, sailed from the Barbary Coast in the southern Mediterranean and raided European trade vessels during the time of the Crusades. Then counter-corsairs subsidized by the Knights of Malta were sent forth to battle the Barbary pirates.

Pirates were given a stamp of respectability and legitimacy by the British king beginning in the thirteenth century with "letters of marque." Renamed privateers, they were allowed to "legally" plunder enemy ships. After those letters of marque were withdrawn by King James I in 1603, privateers gave way to wild buccaneers, who kept only to their own code.

This was really the beginning of the golden age of piracy, which saw its most famous names roaming the Caribbean and having their way with the European powers then holding sway. Their rule over the seas lasted until the nineteenth century, when a lethal combination of technology (the advent of steam power, giving the navies of Britain and the United States the upper hand over sailing ships) and treaties (such as the Declaration of Paris, which banned letters of marque) helped put an end, once and for all, to most piracy.

They may have been cruel, crude, and altogether nasty, but they were towering figures in the chronicles of villainy. Captain Edward Teach, better known as Blackbeard, would place lit matches and slow-burning fuses beneath his hat, setting forth black smoke around his head that would terrify his victims. Captain "Calico Jack" Rackham was so named because of his colorful calico cotton attire.

ABOVE: *Marooned* (1909) by Howard Pyle, whose evocative artwork influenced everyone on the Pirates crew.

"What could be more fun than being a pirate, or at least being a pirate in the movies?" —JERRY BRUCKHEIMER

He joined female pirates Anne Bonny and Mary Read in a life of wanton crime as sort of an eighteenth-century Bonnie, Bonnie, and Clyde. Madame Ching Shih controlled all coastal trade around early nineteenth-century China with her fleet of 1,800 junks and 80,000 men and women. Jean Lafitte, who ran his own pirate kingdom of Barataria, helped General Andrew Jackson defeat the British at the Battle of New Orleans and has a town and national park named for him in Louisiana. Bartholomew "Black Bart" Roberts began his career as a merchant navyman. After his ship was captured by pirates, his own abductors, admiring his intelligence and abilities, elected him their captain. Edward Low was an Englishman so cruel that his own pirate crew mutinied and shipped him out to sea in a rowboat without food or drink. Unfortunately for them, he was rescued the very next day.

And yet, despite the harsh, often brutal realities of piracy through the ages, the public has maintained an often romantic fascination with pirates that has transcended historical truth. Every boy and plenty of girls have at some point dreamed of being a pirate, wild and free, dueling on the yardarm, dagger clenched between the teeth, swinging from one ship to another or digging for buried treasure on a deserted island. This is where reality ends, and mythology, so important to the human condition, takes over. We believe in the romantic mythology of pirates because we need to.

"I think the appeal of piracy to both adults and children," explains historian Peter Twist, who served as technical adviser on the Pirates films, "is based in rebellion against authority. Poor people in the eighteenth century led nasty, short lives with no hope of improvement. Piracy offered a chance to win the lottery. The prospect of punishment was likely rarely considered, and if it was, the rewards were worth the risks. I believe that pirates have been romanticized in the same way and for the same reasons that gunslingers were in the Old West. They led thrilling, extraordinary lives. The fact that they were also short lives is largely overlooked."

"Most people are condemned to lives of monotony," writes David Cordingly in his book *Under the Black Flag: The Romance and the Reality of Life Among the Pirates*. "The pirates escaped from the laws and regulations that govern most of us. They were rebels against authority, free spirits who made up their own rules. They left behind the gray world of rainswept streets and headed for the sun. We imagine them sprawled on sandy beaches, with a bottle of rum in one hand, a lovely woman by their side, and a sleek black schooner moored offshore waiting to carry them away to distant and exotic islands."

Readers and audiences were enthusiastic to buy into this fantasy, as were writers. The great Romantic George Gordon, Lord Byron, was partially responsible for creating much of the mythology in his 1814 poem *The Corsair*. The fact that real pirates were still terrorizing British sailors in the Caribbean did little to dissuade Byron's swooning readers, who were so mesmerized by his tale of a pirate captain who risked his one true love and his own life to save a slave in a Turkish harem, that its entire first printing sold out on the first day of publication in London.

"To be a pirate—it's a childhood dream, isn't it?
To basically get away with everything . . .
and get paid for it!"

—JOHNNY DEPP

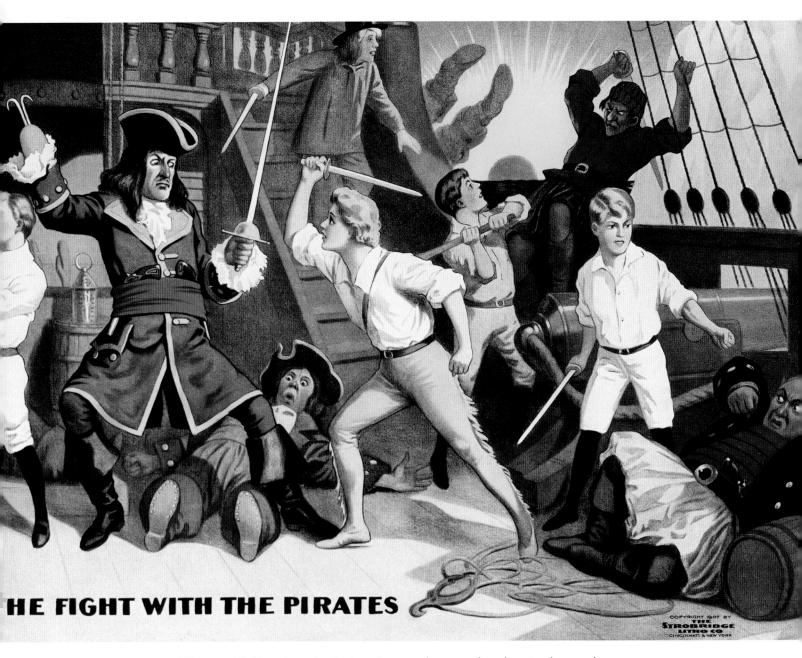

HE FIGHT WITH THE PIRATES

COPYRIGHT 1907 BY
THE
STROBRIDGE
LITHO CO
CINCINNATI & NEW YORK

Gilbert and Sullivan brought singing pirates to the stage when they simultaneously premiered *The Pirates of Penzance, or The Slave of Duty* in both Britain and America on New Year's Eve, 1879. But it was Scottish writer Robert Louis Stevenson who helped seal much of the iconography to be seen in future books, plays, and films when he wrote *Treasure Island* in 1883. His fictional peg-legged pirate Long John Silver, parrot firmly perched on shoulder, became the yardstick by which all other such characters were measured. In 1903, American illustrator Howard Pyle created some of the most enduring images of the pirate's life in his wonderful *Book of Pirates*, tremendously influencing the visual perception of pirate lore and legend (including Pirates of the Caribbean director Gore Verbinski, a passionate admirer of Pyle's work). In another piratical product of the Edwardian era, *Peter Pan* writer J.M. Barrie (who, coincidentally, Johnny Depp would brilliantly portray in the excellent 2004 film *Finding Neverland*) invented—initially for the stage and then in a prose version—another pirate legend in the deliciously neurotic and contemptible Captain Hook. By this time, it seems, the public's conception of real-life pirates had segued from terrifying psychopaths of the seas to an almost nostalgic remembrance of things past.

ABOVE: Theatrical poster advertising "Fight with the Pirates" from *Peter Pan*, published by Strobridge, 1907.

*"There's something primal about pirates.
For me, pirate movies have always been about
characters obtaining their desires—ultimately through
piracy—and the good and bad that comes with it."*

—GORE VERBINSKI

Then came the pirate movies and for a good long while they came endlessly. From the sublime to the ridiculous, these films were an escapist staple of the medium, luring children and grown-ups alike with timeless tales of bravery and cowardice, crime and punishment, nobles and knaves. Two kids growing up in different parts of America were no different than their counterparts elsewhere in the world. "I certainly had my favorite pirate movies as a kid," says Jerry Bruckheimer. "*The Crimson Pirate, Captain Blood, The Black Pirate, The Black Swan, Treasure Island*—all classics of swashbuckling and skullduggery. What could be more fun than being a pirate, or at least being a pirate in the movies? They were freewheeling, rebellious, unafraid to defy authority."

Gore Verbinski was also a devotee of pirate movies, especially *Captain Blood* and *The Crimson Pirate*, featuring Errol Flynn (in the former) and Burt Lancaster (in the latter) performing thrilling, acrobatic feats of courageous derring-do. "We like pirates for the same reason that we like Sid Vicious," says the director, alluding to his own punk rock roots. "There's something primal about pirates. For me, pirate movies have always been about characters obtaining their desires—ultimately through piracy—and the good and bad that comes with it."

The catalogue of pirate movies is voluminous and international, from such classics as the aforementioned *The Black Pirate* (1926), *Captain Blood* (1935), and *The Crimson Pirate* (1952) to several highly romanticized versions of Jean Lafitte's story, including two versions produced by Cecil B. DeMille in 1938 and 1958 (*The Buccaneer*). There are at least twenty-five different versions of Stevenson's *Treasure Island* and such low-budget contributions as *Abbott and Costello Meet Captain Kidd* (1952), *Morgan the Pirate* (1961), *Pirates of Tortuga* (1961), and *Rage of the Buccaneers* (1962). A series of Italian movies in the 1960s and an even more popular 1976 TV series were both based on Emilio Salgari's popular nineteenth century novel *Sandokan, The Tiger of Malaysia*, which detoured from the usual Caribbean settings to Southeast Asia. Nor were ancient pirates ignored in the movies. Charlton Heston, who twenty-one years later would portray Long John Silver in a television version of *Treasure Island*, battled Macedonian raiders attacking the Roman galley in which he was enslaved in *Ben-Hur* (1959). As Spartacus in Stanley Kubrick's 1960 epic, Kirk Douglas made an arrangement with the shady, multi-ringed, Middle Eastern pirate Tigranes Levantus (Herbert Lom) for his army of runaway slaves to be returned to their various home countries. Of course, being a pirate, Tigranes ultimately betrayed Spartacus to save his own skin. As Captain Jack Sparrow would prove many years later, you have to watch out for pirates with multiple rings on their fingers.

Besides 1950's *Treasure Island*, the Walt Disney Studios also featured pirates in its classic 1960 adventure *Swiss Family Robinson*; the comic fantasy

OPPOSITE: Poster for *The Black Swan*, based on the classic Rafael Sabatini adventure.

29

Blackbeard's Ghost (1968) with Peter Ustinov in the title role; the 1990 Norwegian-made seafaring adventure *Shipwrecked* (aka *Haakon Haakonsen*, the name of the lad who is the tale's central figure); the animated feature *Peter Pan* (1953) and its made-for-video sequel *Return to Never Land* (2002); and *Treasure Planet* (2002), a futuristic, science-fiction adaptation of the Stevenson novel.

Through these legends, myths, movies, plays, and books, we live out our own fantasies of waving the skull and crossbones, untethered from historical veracity perhaps, but strongly connected to an almost genetic yearning for absolute freedom. Because as Johnny Depp puts it, "To be a pirate—it's a childhood dream, isn't it? To basically get away with everything . . . and get paid for it!"

When movies turned to space wars and comic book heroes, and filmmakers seemed to lose their swashbuckling edge, contemporary audiences lost interest in these piratanical entertainments, except for the Disney theme park attraction that never lacked for those eager to sail through its picaresque adventures. And just as the Pirates of the Caribbean attraction had successfully propagated the notion of piracy as good, if grubby, fun, it was time to restore the pirate motion picture genre to its rightful place in movie history. At the head of the fleet.

BELOW: *Treasure Island* was the Walt Disney Studios first feature-length live-action film.

The world's greatest rogue and a tough young cabin boy match wits in a dangerous game!

WALT DISNEY

presents

Treasure Island

Robert Louis Stevenson's rousing adventure!

BOBBY DRISCOLL ROBERT NEWTON
BASIL SYDNEY

TECHNICOLOR®

Produced by
PERCE PEARCE

Directed by
BYRON HASKIN

Screenplay by
LAWRENCE E. WATKIN · Re-released by Buena Vista Distribution Co., Inc. © 1975 Walt Disney Productions G

PASSING THE PIRATES TORCH

I have great memories of going on that ride when I was a little kid, because when you're a little kid all you want to be is a pirate. I'd go on it endlessly, bore the tears out of everyone else to just continue riding it. And now, as an adult, it's fantastic to go back and take my kids on the ride."

The source of that quote? Johnny Depp. And how impossible it would have been for that little boy to know that one day he himself, in the character of Captain Jack Sparrow, would be transformed into an Audio-Animatronics character by the wizards at Walt Disney Imagineering and inserted into the very ride he loved so much, when Pirates of the Caribbean was revised in concert with the opening of *Pirates of the Caribbean: Dead Man's Chest* in 2006.

After nearly 40 years of continuous operation, the Pirates of the Caribbean attraction is more than a Disney classic—it is a legacy, one of the last rides in which Walt Disney personally had a hand in conceiving and designing. The attraction was a twinkle in Walt's eye as early as 1954, conceived originally as a walk-through wax museum in New Orleans Square, but it was not fully developed until the early 1960s. Some of the greatest minds in WED Enterprises (the former moniker of Disney's great creative think tank, standing for **W**alter **E**lias **D**isney, before it became Walt Disney Imagineering in 1986) had a hand in the development and design

ABOVE: Visual development art by Bruce Bushman for the Pirates attraction; BELOW: Herb Ryman's 1965 concept art of the jail scene.

31

NEW ORLEANS SQUARE

ABOVE: Poster for the 1967 Pirates of the Caribbean attraction premiere by Marc Davis; RIGHT: Walt Disney examines a scale model of the Burning Town scene with Imagineer Claude Coats.

of New Orleans Square, including Sam McKim, Duane Alt, Dorothea Redmond, and Herb Ryman. Construction finally began in 1961, but two years later all that existed of the proposed Pirate Wax Museum was a huge empty basement. Handed the primary assignment of designing the pirate figures was Marc Davis, who started at Disney in 1935 as an apprentice animator on *Snow White and the Seven Dwarfs* and ultimately became one of Walt's "Nine Old Men" of animation.

What changed the walk-through concept of the Pirate Wax Museum was something at which Disney had always excelled—technology. The brilliant robotics that the Imagineers developed had emerged with its own special name: Audio-Animatronics. This was first applied to animals featured in both the Jungle Cruise in Adventureland and the Mine Train Through Nature's Wonderland attraction in Frontierland, but was about to make a bigger splash in the first all Audio-Animatronics show, The Enchanted Tiki Room. Disney and his Imagineers took this new world in conceptual entertainment to greater heights with the four attractions they developed for the 1964–1965 New York World's Fair: the Magic Skyway, which featured lifelike dinosaurs as viewed from a moving Ford motor car; "it's a small world," where children and animals of the world danced and played for appreciative crowds floating past in small boats; the Carousel of Progress, which applied Audio-Animatronics to more realistic human figures (and during which the audience rotated around a circular stage, rather than the stage itself moving); and most astonishingly, perhaps, Lincoln in the Illinois pavilion—later known in Disneyland as "Great Moments with Mr. Lincoln"—where an amazingly lifelike sixteenth president rose from a seated position and addressed the audience.

The die was cast. The Pirate Wax Museum would now be Pirates of the Caribbean, a ride-through environment populated by fully articulated, state-of-the-art Audio-Animatronics figures. Marc Davis and Blaine Gibson designed the characters and Claude Coats designed the settings. What emerged, under the supervision of WED president Richard (Dick) Irvine, a former Hollywood art director, was a revolutionary combination of thrills, chills, and laughs that raised

the bar for theme park rides forever. Generations of guests have merrily taken the ride, humming (or singing aloud) the attraction's theme song, "Yo Ho (A Pirate's Life For Me)," written by composer George Bruns with lyrics provided by the attraction's scriptwriter, Francis "X" Atencio.

Pirates of the Caribbean officially opened on April 19, 1967, but sadly, Walt Disney was not to be in attendance. The great man had passed away on December 15, 1966. It's a tribute to Walt that the last attraction in which he had a personal hand was a monumental success, first at Disneyland, then at Walt Disney World in Orlando, where a slightly altered version opened on December 15, 1973, exactly seven years to the day after Walt's death. Pirates of the Caribbean attractions followed at Tokyo Disneyland in 1983 and Disneyland Resort Paris (formerly EuroDisney) in 1992, also tremendous hits with the parks' guests.

RIGHT: Marc Davis's original illustration of the Pooped Pirate; BELOW: Johnny Depp enjoys a face-to-face meeting with the Audio-Animatronics version of himself as Captain Jack Sparrow, accompanied by the latest incarnation of the Pooped Pirate.

In 2006, Captain Jack Sparrow, Captain Barbossa, and Davy Jones seamlessly slipped alongside the Audio-Animatronics characters that Disneyphiles had come to know and love so much for the past forty years. Spearheading the enhancement, which opened to enthusiastic response from even the most traditional of fans, was a whole new generation of Imagineers, including WDI's senior vice president creative development, Eric Jacobson, senior show producer Kathy Rogers, senior concept writer Michael Sprout, director/concept designer Chris Turner, chief sculptor Valerie Edwards, principal show animator John Cutry, and principal character concept designer Doug Griffith.

The Man Behind the Lightning Bolt

The story of the Pirates of the Caribbean journey from concept to reality, first as a world-famous theme park attraction, then as one of the most successful film franchises of all time, is also the story of how people of vision turn dreams into reality by making the right moves at the right times and by working with vast teams of creative artists who share their excitement.

Like Walt Disney, Jerry Bruckheimer has spun an empire of dreams focused on the fine art of entertaining millions of people. Also like Walt, he has an infallible faith not only in the American dream and its limitless possibilities, but also in the certainty that those dreams can and do come true. And, like Walt Disney, Jerry Bruckheimer has brought a maverick spirit into mainstream Hollywood entertainment.

First and foremost, Bruckheimer believes in the power of a good story with strong characters. He also believes in utilizing technology to support that notion, rather than the other way around. He is the proud populist of the contemporary film and television industry, with a deep understanding of and abiding love for what has mesmerized audiences since the dawn of the medium. "Men and women have always gone to the movies to be dazzled by million-dollar productions that tantalize the senses and expand the imagination," notes Bruckheimer. However, the producer insists that he doesn't try to "guess" the audiences' taste. Instead, he says, "I make movies based on gut. I only make movies that I want to see." And since he has always taken a determinedly non-elitist stance—describing himself as a "mainstream, cheeseburger kind of guy"—Jerry Bruckheimer knows what audiences like because, very simply, the two entities are inseparable. Bruckheimer doesn't have to take wild swings in the dark at what audiences like—he *is* the audience, an avid moviegoer since his childhood days in Detroit, Michigan.

His first films were actually the sixty-second tales he told as an award-winning commercial producer in Detroit, one of which—a parody of *Bonnie and Clyde* created for Pontiac and noted for its brilliance in *Time* magazine—brought the 23-year-old producer to the attention of world-renowned ad agency BBD&O, who lured him to New York City. Four years on Madison Avenue gave him the experience and confidence to tackle Hollywood, and there, not yet thirty, he produced his first film, *Farewell, My Lovely.*

BELOW: Jerry Bruckheimer on the massive Singapore set of *At World's End.*

Bruckheimer's films and television series have not only influenced popular culture, but in many cases, defined it. And although cinema has been considered a director's medium since the French popularized the auteur theory, Bruckheimer has put an indelible stamp on his film and television productions that hearkens back to the days of such strong, creative, hands-on producers as David O. Selznick (*Gone With The Wind*), Darryl F. Zanuck (*The Longest Day*), Sam Spiegel (*Lawrence of Arabia*) and, for that matter, Walt Disney himself. These were all fearless pioneers who were unafraid to go and go big when the situation or subject matter warranted that approach. More than any other contemporary producer, Jerry Bruckheimer has not only become a household name, but an actual brand.

That lightning bolt in Jerry Bruckheimer Films' now familiar logo has struck not twice, but countless times. The titles of Bruckheimer's films, first with his late partner Don Simpson and then on his own, segue from one blockbuster to the next:

American Gigolo, Flashdance, Top Gun, Days of Thunder, Beverly Hills Cop, Bad Boys, Crimson Tide, The Rock, Con Air, Armageddon, Enemy of the State, Remember the Titans, Pearl Harbor, Black Hawk Down, National Treasure, King Arthur, and, of course, the Pirates of the Caribbean films. At the same time, Bruckheimer has also nurtured more intimate film fare such as _Dangerous Minds, Veronica Guerin,_ and _Glory Road_ that have pondered political and social themes with considerable courage and insight. His television work, including _C.S.I., C.S.I.: Miami, C.S.I.: NY, Without A Trace, Cold Case, The Amazing Race,_ and many others, has brought cinematic, feature film–like qualities to the small screen.

ABOVE: Johnny Depp and Jerry Bruckheimer chat on set.

And the audience has spoken, loudly: Bruckheimer's films have earned worldwide revenues of over $14.4 billion in box office and home entertainment receipts. In the 2005–2006 network television season, he produced eight series, a feat unprecedented in nearly sixty years of television history. His work has been acknowledged with thirty-nine Academy Award nominations, five Academy Awards, twenty-three Golden Globe nominations, four Golden Globes, fifty-three Emmy Award nominations, fourteen Emmys, sixteen People's Choice nominations, eleven People's Choice awards, five Grammys, fourteen _Teen People_ Teen Choice awards, and numerous MTV awards, including one for Best Picture of the Decade (_Beverly Hills Cop_). _Variety_ named Bruckheimer "Showman of the Year" in its July 10, 2006, edition.

The surprisingly reserved, modest, even shy Bruckheimer has never been one to rest on his laurels. Instead, the man behind the lightning bolt relentlessly surges into the future. "I don't look back and celebrate," he notes. "I just always worry about the next one."

The stars of Pirates all agree that there is nothing like being on the set of a Jerry Bruckheimer film. "There's always a sense of 'how can we be better?' that's part of Jerry's attitude toward life and moviemaking: that there's nothing you can't do," says Orlando Bloom. "It's a courageous way to make films—fearless and sometimes a little overwhelming."

"I've done four films with Jerry now," adds Keira Knightley, "and it's just amazing. They're really, really big! The scale of these movies is just huge. Jerry has created an entire pirate world, and we're all part of it. It's fantastic."

"The first film felt very intimate and got more and more grand as time went on," says Johnny Depp. "The second and third were just totally, utterly Jerry Bruckheimer, which means that it's very grand but done with incredible taste. Jerry uses the best guys in the business and it's impressive."

"There's always a sense of 'how can we be better?' that's part of Jerry's attitude toward life and moviemaking: that there's nothing you can't do."

—ORLANDO BLOOM

Gore Verbinski: Rebel *with* a Cause

Gore Verbinski was a director I wanted to work with very early in his career," recalls Jerry Bruckheimer of the hugely talented man who would come to helm all three Pirates of the Caribbean epics. "I saw a reel of Gore's commercials and thought that he was really talented. Gore has great storytelling skills, an amazing visual sense, tremendous enthusiasm, and was the perfect director for the Pirates movies."

On set, Verbinski is always focused, always working, little time for small talk—not because he's unfriendly—but because he's fully aware of the task and realizes that there's no time to spare. With his ultra-casual dress (including either a bush hat or pirate-style head scarf) and soft spoken manner, Verbinski does nothing to trumpet the fact that he's now one of the industry's most successful directors. To his colleagues on set, though, Verbinski's quiet authority speaks volumes, gaining their respect, their loyalty, and perhaps most importantly, their friendship.

Gore Verbinski is a true anomaly in Hollywood: a man who works within the system, and with massive success, but is also independent-minded to the

OPPOSITE: Gore Verbinski and his storyboard "scribblings" on location in the Pelegostos Village set on the island of Dominica; ABOVE: Verbinski works in rainy conditions with Geoffrey Rush and Johnny Depp.

37

core, with a vast knowledge of film history and a tremendous love of the medium. In his previous vocation, Verbinski was a guitarist with such seminal punk bands as The Daredevils and Little Kings, and although he in no way strikes anyone as a hell-raiser, the director is clearly attracted to the notion of breaking rules, pushing the envelope, and in general shaking things up for the betterment of the film in particular, and the art form in general.

What originally attracted Verbinski to Pirates of the Caribbean? "Just the concept," is his response. "My agent called and said 'How do you feel about a pirate movie?' I mean, how often are you going to get that call? It's sort of the singularly most failed genre of our time, but I thought it had to be attempted one more time. I think there's something rebellious about pirates, something revolutionary about them. They came out of a time when things were oppressive; you could get hung for stealing a loaf of bread. For me, the Pirates films are about when it's right to break rules to achieve what you want."

After graduating from UCLA, the filmmaker became an award-winning commercial director, honored with four Clio Awards and a Cannes Silver Lion award for his work on an assortment of memorable advertising spots, including the first of the popular Budweiser "Frog" spots. True to his rock roots, Verbinski also directed music videos for such cutting-edge artists as Bad Religion, L7, and The Crystal Method.

His first film, *Mouse Hunt,* converted what could have been just a cute little movie about two brothers chasing an elusive mouse in a musty old mansion into a strongly visual and surprisingly edgy walk on the wild side, albeit one still suitable for young audiences. It also demonstrated the kind of complex, Rube Goldberg-esque physical action that would later delight audiences in the Pirates films. *The Mexican* was a romantic comedy-thriller that paid stylistic homage to "spaghetti western" maestro Sergio Leone, one of Verbinski's favorite directors, while further establishing his fearless melding of different genres. *The Ring,* based on a Japanese horror movie, outdid the original by creating a powerful atmosphere of pure, poetic dread. Never one to follow marked paths, in between the release of *Pirates of the Caribbean: The Curse of the Black Pearl* and the filming of the next two adventures, Verbinski turned his attention to intimate drama with *The Weather Man,* a strong examination of thwarted American dreams and unexpected redemption.

The Curse of the Black Pearl was enough of an epic challenge for the young director, but taking on the simultaneous and back-to-back filming of *Dead Man's Chest* and *At World's End* was a gargantuan task that would give pause to even the most grizzled industry veterans. From the time preparations began on *Dead Man's Chest* in June 2004, until *At World's End* was put to bed just before its release in late May 2007, Verbinski worked 24/7, with scant (if any) days off—conditions that would melt down the toughest directors. When asked by a journalist what his plans were after completing *At World's End,* Verbinski jokingly responded "I'm going to move to the mountains and raise goats."

Says Johnny Depp, "I have a profound respect for Gore, and always have since the first instant we worked together on the first film. Watching what he had to deal with on the Pirates movies was incredible. With the kind of pressure he was working under, I never saw him step outside or lose his composure, or his vision. He just sort of deals and fights his way out of that corner."

Facing a barrage of every conceivable challenge, whether technical or meteorological, Gore Verbinski would repeat, with tongue considerably wedged in cheek, a rueful line that became something of a mantra to get him through the days, weeks, months, and years of filming the Pirates of the Caribbean films: "Everything is going according to plan."

OPPOSITE: Half-shrouded in smoke, Gore Verbinski directs from the "210" dock on Grand Bahama Island.

624

A PISTOL SHOT rings out -- and Akshay stiffens, falls over.
Everyone looks over -- except Jack.

Behind him stands CAPTAIN TEAGUE in a doorway, gunslinger
pose, smoke still rising from his pistol.

React to Teague   (Reshoot)

                    TEAGUE
          The Code is the law.

Hand on the butt of a second pistol, he stares at Sumbhajee.
Sumbhajee gestures to Pusan to step into Ashay's place. Pusan
looks nervous as Sambhajee gestures again -- and then greatly
relieved.

Slowly crane   Push to Schun

                    PUSAN
Sri Sambhajee explains that a great
misunderstanding has occurred, and
avers that indeed the Code is the
Law.

en Teague and the table

                    TEAGUE
          You're in my way, boy.

look at him ... then steps aside as two pirates
Manuscript into the room -- THE CODE.

                    PINTEL
          (with awe, to Ragetti)
          The Code!

                    RAGETTI
          (with awe, to Pintel)
          As set forth by Morgan and
          Bartholomew!

whistles -- and the PRISON DOG runs into the room,
ing in his mouth. Pintel and Ragetti recognize him --

                    PINTEL
          It be the same pooch, can

Surrounded By Scribbles

It may seem a bit odd, but from the moment of conception, I intuitively begin to deconstruct an idea into a series of shots. This fragmentation is an essential part of the process, allowing me to break apart the greater thing into adjustable parts that I can use and control. I then rebuild the narrative into what I refer to as the "shot construct" (the sequencing of the images). This is the vehicle that delivers a particular idea or concept to the screen, giving it specificity, voice and intention.

I try to scribble the shots down loosely and quickly in order to keep ideas fluid and malleable. This becomes the vocabulary of the film for me, and my office, trailer, and script are swimming in them. They're useful to remind me down the road what my original intention might have been, or to impart upon the crew a specific way we are going to shoot a scene.

The "shot construct" occasionally becomes the source of some debate, because although clear to me, the sketches or "thumbnails" can sometimes be indecipherable to others. More than once I have witnessed a crew member holding my best work upside down and uttering something to the effect of "Is that a foot?"

I often have these scribbles redrawn into storyboard form for the sake of clarity. My good friend Jim Byrkit contributes both his ideas and his substantial artistry in this process. From time to time I have asked my seven- and ten-year-old sons, Anton and Ivan, to review my work. But in the end, it is the language I use, and along with muttered sound effects and a badly hummed musical idea, it usually conveys what is going on inside my head.

—Gore Verbinski

Launching the Pirates' Voyage

The writing team of Ted Elliott and Terry Rossio share several qualities with director Gore Verbinski: deep intellect, a bottomless pit of dry and sometimes outrageous humor, a love of complex stories with constant surprises and unexpected bends in the road, and a supernatural capacity for hard work on a daily basis. Throughout production of all three films, Verbinski, Elliott, and Rossio would relentlessly pick over the scripts, with the minute attention to detail of serious scholars, which may come as something of a surprise considering the often lighthearted, rambunctious humor of the Pirates movies. "There's no heavier burden than great potential," sighed Elliott at one point during filming of *Dead Man's Chest* on Grand Bahama Island, quoting that great American philosopher, Charlie Brown. From the time they set sail on *The Curse of the Black Pearl*, to the final moments of *At World's End*, Verbinski, Bruckheimer, Elliott, and Rossio were always aware of how high the expectations were for the Pirates films, and were absolutely determined not to take the easy way out.

The Pirates films weren't even a speck on the horizon back in 1992, when Elliott and Rossio—who had just enjoyed a major success by scribing *Aladdin*—pitched a film version of the Pirates of the Caribbean attraction to production executives at the Walt Disney Studios. Considering the bleached bones of pirate films that had washed up on the shores of Hollywood in the previous decade, it's not surprising that the studio chose to pass. Eight years later, in the spring of 2000, the studio revisited the notion of converting various attractions into feature films. Elliott and Rossio were the studio's first choice to write the Pirates film but they were unavailable, not to be unexpected considering their growing demand, having subsequently written such blockbusters as *Shrek* and *The Mask of Zorro*. The studio then called upon the screenwriting talents of Jay Wolpert, who had recently written the excellent retro-swashbuckler *The Count of Monte Cristo* for the studio's Touchstone Pictures. Another draft of the script followed by Stuart Beattie, who was soon to write Michael Mann's taut thriller *Collateral*.

When it became time to find the right producer for the project, Dick Cook, chairman, The Walt Disney Studios, and Nina Jacobson, president, Buena Vista Motion Pictures Group, knew just the man—the same guy who had been turning out hit after hit for the Studio for years and had forged a position as the foremost producer of his time.

Jerry Bruckheimer's first response, however, was not altogether encouraging. "I thought about it and said that I didn't want to make a movie based on an

LEFT: Screenwriters Ted Elliott and Terry Rossio photographed beneath the Jolly Roger on Grand Bahama Island; OPPOSITE: Visual consultant James Ward Byrkit's development art of Captain Jack Sparrow's now-famous first appearance in *The Curse of the Black Pearl*, executed before Johnny Depp was cast in the role.

"It was Ted and Terry who took the supernatural element of the ride and applied it to the story, creating the idea of cursed pirates, which was the little edge that made me think that this was something that was really special."

—JERRY BRUCKHEIMER

attraction, that it really didn't interest me. But I read the script, and felt that although it was too linear and lacked the pizzazz that I like to give to an audience, there were possibilities." Mike Stenson and Chad Oman, the crack team that heads the feature production department at Jerry Bruckheimer Films brought the finally available team of Rossio and Elliott to Bruckheimer's attention. Thus began a long and fruitful collaboration that would see both Stenson and Oman involved every step of the way with the development not only of *The Curse of the Black Pearl* script, but the screenplays for *Dead Man's Chest* and *At World's End* as well.

"Ted and Terry are wonderful writers," says Bruckheimer, "who came in with an element of the movie that really excited and made me want to see it—and if I want to see it, I want to make it—which was the supernatural. It was Ted and Terry who took the supernatural element of the ride and applied it to the story, creating the idea of cursed pirates, which was the little edge that made me think that this was something really special."

After more than a decade of languishing, Pirates of the Caribbean was finally up and running as a major feature film. Quips Terry Rossio, "At least we had ten years to think about what we wanted to do with the movie," alluding to their original pitch to the studio. "So when it came back around, I think we were kind of ready."

BELOW: Conceptual illustration by Simon Murton.

Elliott and Rossio were determined to utilize elements of the Pirates of the Caribbean attraction in their screen story, as both were longtime fans. "What

we wanted to do was to come up with a story that would affect people in much the same way that the attraction affected us the first time we rode it," says Elliott. "And we had to do it across an entire age spectrum."

"The films are really derived from the spirit of the attraction," adds Rossio. "And the ride also provides a narrative, with dramatic turns and escalating conflict. Our hope was that people would find the same spirit of excitement, fear, and humor in the movie."

The story of what finally emerged as *Pirates of the Caribbean: The Curse of the Black Pearl* went through the several revisions that are an integral part of the Hollywood process. In the original story as composed by Disney executive Brigham Taylor, creative executive Michael Haines, and Josh Harmon of the studio's story department, Will, a prison guard, sets out to rescue Elizabeth, the Governor's daughter, when she's kidnapped and held for ransom by a pirate named Black-heart. In order to save her, Will must link fortunes with Jack, a former member of Blackheart's pirate crew.

That version was developed and refined by Jay Wolpert, who introduced some real-life pirate figures in cameo appearances. Stuart Beattie added the characters of Commodore Norrington (replacing a villainous Captain of the Guard named Defoe in the original story), Captain Wraith (replacing Blackheart), and the ornithological surnames of Elizabeth and Jack: Swann and Sparrow.

Elliott and Rossio built upon what Jay Wolpert and Stuart Beattie had

ABOVE LEFT AND RIGHT: In a direct reference to the attraction, the jailed pirates attempt to entice the Prison Dog, who literally holds the keys to their freedom; BELOW: Twigg in skeletal form, one of the cursed *Black Pearl* pirates.

already contributed rather than go back to square one, because, as Rossio realized, "there was a lot of good material there." The story was now laced with supernatural elements, such as the notion of the cursed Aztec gold and what it's done to the *Black Pearl* and her unfortunate crew; they unseated Captain Wraith/Blackheart with a new character named Barbossa; inserted several intentional moments that directly reflected the Pirates attraction; and while retaining the romantic flourishes of the previous drafts, refined and polished the story until it positively gleamed with possibilities for truly original big-screen entertainment. Notes Elliott, "The entire idea of the cursed treasure and pirates comes from the moment you begin the ride and the voice says, 'No fear of evil curses says ye. Properly warned ye be, says I.'"

Elliott and Rossio were also shaping and forming—on the written page, anyway—the character of Captain Jack Sparrow. "We wanted Jack to be a character who the audience never quite knows—is he good or bad? Is he a great pirate or the luckiest bad pirate who ever lived?" The writers graced Captain Sparrow with what has found its place among the great character introductions in all movie history: "In the opening, you see Jack in all his swashbuckling glory as he's sailing into harbor," explains Elliott. "And then you realize he's on the crappiest little boat you've ever seen. It literally sinks beneath him. Jack is someone who needs a ship badly, but even as the craft drops below the water, he still strikes the heroic pose. Jack understands the importance of image better than anybody."

Elliott and Rossio imagined Captain Jack to be part of a long and distinguished literary tradition. "One archetype that is really underused in American cinema," notes Rossio, "is the trickster character. Most American movies tend to celebrate the warrior who does the right thing at the right time. But the fun thing about Jack, who is definitely a trickster, is that he's not particularly good at avoiding getting caught. He will get caught, you just can't hold on to him for very long. Jack knows that if he can bide his time, eventually the world will come over to his side, and that gives him this sort of supreme confidence that he can handle just about any situation."

BELOW: Captain Barbossa occupying Captain Sparrow's cabin on the *Black Pearl*.

"The other fun thing about the trickster character," continues Elliott, "is that he is basically just out to have his own good time. He's following his own self interests. The things he does will affect other people—the mortals, if you will—

and sometimes it will be to a good benefit, and sometimes it will be to their detriment. So that goes back to the question posed in all three movies: is Jack Sparrow a good guy or is he a bad guy? Is he a pirate hero or pirate villain? Well, it really kind of depends on the perspective you have."

When Elliott and Rossio presented Gore Verbinski with their take on the tale, the director was enthusiastic. "It was a terrific perversion of the classic tale," he recalls. "I came in asking, 'What is the standard plot structure? Is it a kidnapping? Is it buried treasure?' When actually, it has all of these qualities, yet the principle one is reversed. It is a film about finding the last piece of treasure and putting it back. Barbossa and his pirates need to return the last piece of cursed treasure so they can feel the pleasures of the flesh-and-blood world. The curse has allowed Barbossa and his pirates to keep the currency and to continue their villainy, but they're not able to enjoy it."

"The second I heard that Ted and Terry were going to be writing the film," says Johnny Depp, "I knew we were in great shape, in addition to Gore directing. I knew that there would be strong shoulders for the project to stand on. And when I read the screenplay I was pleasantly surprised, even beyond my expectations, because they brought such a great amount of humor to it."

Pirates of the Caribbean: The Curse of the Black Pearl was an authentic smash sleeper hit, an adventure/comedy/fantasy/swashbuckler that melted one genre into another with alarming ease, creating enduring characters and witty, highly literate dialogue.

When the time came for the filmmakers to tackle *Pirates of the Caribbean: Dead Man's Chest* and *Pirates of the Caribbean: At World's End*, Bruckheimer, Verbinski, Elliott, and Rossio all knew what they didn't want to do—repeat themselves.

Filmmaking is a collaborative art, and in addition to Verbinski and Bruckheimer, there were others involved in developing the meticulous details that went into the three Pirates films. Particularly important in the process was creative consultant James Ward Byrkit, who first worked with Gore on *Mouse Hunt* as a storyboard artist. "We would spitball ideas back and forth over endless cups of coffee in the middle of the night," recalls Verbinski, "which is how movies really get made." Verbinski and Byrkit conceived in their physical minutiae several of the amazingly complex sequences, translating their concepts to storyboards, from which Verbinski worked on set throughout shooting. Endless script meetings were

ABOVE: Will Turner watches as a confident Captain Jack effects a plot to take the *Dauntless* in *The Curse of the Black Pearl*; OVERLEAF: Captain Jack and the "thump thump"—the beating heart of Davy Jones.

held by the filmmakers and the writers in what Verbinski calls "the war room," a diminutive office lined with sketches, illustrations, and index cards representing each scene that could be rearranged as the screenplays developed.

"You really need to have some substance behind it to do a story that spans three films," confirms executive producer Mike Stenson of Jerry Bruckheimer Films. "You need to not only deliver the entertainment value, the roller coaster ride, and the laughs, but if you're going to ask people to stay around for three movies, you have to feel like there's something thematically significant that you're going to explore."

"Whereas in the first film, the theme park attraction was a wellspring for ideas, for the second and third films we actually went back to the first movie," notes Rossio. Adds Elliott, "There was a richness to the characters that we felt we could explore, but you don't want to just go through the same paces with the characters. You don't want to see them doing the same thing. One of the things we liked about the characters in the first film was that there's a certain moral ambiguity to them, and we wanted to explore that. We wanted to put Jack Sparrow into a situation where he has to do something that, in fact, puts his goals in opposition to Will and Elizabeth's goals. It was all about expanding the characters and taking them in a farther direction."

"Similarly," continues Rossio, "much of the basis of the first movie was the romantic story between Will and Elizabeth, and we knew we wanted to get into more of a mature examination of the relationship between the two of them. What happens to Will and Elizabeth after that wildly romantic final kiss with the beautiful sunset at the end of *The Curse of the Black Pearl*?"

Taking the supernatural thread several steps further, *Dead Man's Chest* and *At World's End* also dip deeply into the treasure trove of pirate and seagoing lore and mythology, from Davy Jones, he of the famous "locker," to the legendary Kraken, a sea monster fabled since twelfth century Norwegian chronicles. "You think of the sea," says Elliott, "and there are a lot of supernatural stories you've heard. But nobody had actually done those stories as part of a larger pirate movie or swashbuckler, so there was a wealth of legends to draw from. We touched on some of those in the first movie: there's a line of dialogue in which Will talks about sending himself down to Davy Jones's Locker. So in *Dead Man's Chest* and *At World's End*, we decided to explore who Davy Jones is, and then we brought in another well-

ABOVE and OPPOSITE: James Ward Byrkit's illustration of a forlorn Elizabeth Swann at her wedding and Keira Knightley in the "live" image of same in *Dead Man's Chest*.

known legend of the sea, the *Flying Dutchman*, and combined them together."

The filmmakers also cleverly utilized one of history's greatest economic and political powers—the East India Trading Company—as a pivotal entity in the plot of the second and third films. Like much else in the Pirates movies, historical reality is used as a springboard for fun and fantasy. The real British East India Company was a tool of imperialist domination from 1600 to its dissolution in 1858, essentially ruling India and spreading its tentacles as far as the Persian Gulf, Southeast Asia, and East Asia. Even the most generous contemporary histories describe the East India Company's activities as extraordinarily greedy and inhumane. "What we like about pirates," says Elliott, "is that they represent freedom. And the East India Company, as a giant multinational corporation, represents the end of individual freedom. They're defining the world as they want it to be, and there will be a lot of people they're going to leave out. The more dominance they have, the less room there is for people like Captain Jack Sparrow."

By the third film, Bruckheimer, Verbinski, Elliott, and Rossio pushed themselves even farther—quite literally, to the ends of the earth. "What we set for ourselves with Jerry, Gore, Johnny, and everyone else," says Elliott, "was to figure out a way to do two more movies that were of a piece with the first one, and yet still be unique in their own right. What we had to do with each one was, as quickly as we could in the story, satisfy expectations. And then set ourselves the challenge to go past that, and create events that people could never anticipate. Which isn't easy."

In addition to re-acquainting audiences with characters introduced in *The Curse of the Black Pearl*—Captain Jack Sparrow, Will Turner, Elizabeth Swann, James Norrington, Governor Weatherby Swann, Joshamee Gibbs, Pintel and Ragetti, Cotton, Marty, and, in a sensational last-minute surprise appearance, Captain Barbossa—*Dead Man's Chest* introduced such delicious new personages as Davy Jones, Bootstrap Bill Turner, Tia Dalma, and Lord Cutler Beckett and his ruthless enforcer, Mercer. The geographic range of the *At World's End* story expands all the way to old Singapore, where Chinese pirate Captain Sao Feng is introduced. Captain Barbossa, freshly returned from the other side of the pale, takes a front-and-center position in the story; this time in an uneasy alliance with his old nemesis, Jack Sparrow, against the forces of the East India Trading Company. Audiences also get to meet the entire international pirate Brethren Court in their hideaway of Shipwreck City, a rogue's gallery of cutthroats and knaves from all the Seven Seas, including the Keeper of the Code, Captain Teague.

Throughout the three Pirates films, Elliott and Rossio worked in absolute concert with both Verbinski and Bruckheimer, and in a business where most producers and directors would prefer that writers be neither seen nor heard after delivering their scripts, they didn't just sail off into the sunset after depositing their splendid screenplays. Instead, they sailed off with the company to every single location, a constant presence on set, constantly creating and reinventing whenever the need arose. "The reason our writers are on set is because we have such a creative director and cast," explains Jerry Bruckheimer. "They come up with such imaginative ideas, and Ted and Terry can incorporate those into the script before we actually shoot a particular scene. Plus, we're always finding new things and nuances when we film. Ted and Terry are so easy to work with, they love being on location, and they're very fast on their feet."

"One of the blessings that we had on the films was to have Ted and Terry around all the time, to be able to hash things out, decide what works and what doesn't," confirms Johnny Depp. "It's important to allow things to happen in the moment, and it was really great to have a couple of writers who were open to that, but at the same time make sure that you didn't trod on anything important in terms of dialogue or story and didn't jeopardize the integrity of their work."

BELOW: The Pirate Lords assemble in Shipwreck City for the Brethren Court in *At World's End*.

"On Location" April 30, 2003

A perfect example of the collaborative nature of the Pirates filmmakers resulted in Captain Jack Sparrow's deliciously evocative final line of dialogue in *The Curse of the Black Pearl*. Terry Rossio recounts in his "On Location" log of April 30, 2003 that some revised staging for the final scene necessitated some new dialogue for Captain Jack to re-establish himself at the helm of the *Black Pearl*, "a command that was interesting, meaningful, a bit more profound than 'Back to work, mates!'" Elliott went to confer with the captain of the *Lady Washington*, one of *The Curse of the Black Pearl*'s ships, to come up with some authentic nautical commands. Rossio, meanwhile, went to Depp to advise him that some new dialogue was on the way. The rest of the story is taken verbatim from Rossio's actual journal:

I go hook up with Ted on the *Lady Washington*, and they've come up with some possible phrases. There were a few that weren't right at all—chief among them, I recall, was "Put the wind to our aft!" That's just not a line you want to use to end a movie. We all liked the phrase, "To stations! Let go, and haul to run free!" I particularly liked the "run free" part, it seemed appropriate for Depp's character, who considered his ship a symbol of freedom.

So we run the line past Gore, he stares off into the distance, says "I dunno. I get kind of a *Born Free* vibe out of that. Maybe something else?"

So, back to the *Lady Washington*. On the way we get a message from a production assistant via walkie-talkie that Depp wants us to meet him in makeup, but the ship is on the way, so we stop off there first, to try to find another line.

Now, I will always remember this:

We hear a shout, look over, and there's Johnny Depp racing toward us full speed from the make-up trailers, only half in costume, waving a piece of paper over his head. He's shouting—I kid you not—"I've got it! Got it!" He races full speed toward the gangplank, and let me tell you something about gangplanks, they're not very sturdy. Whenever we went across, the production was careful to have a sailor on either end, one to help you on, the other to help you down onto the ship.

Depp wasn't waiting for that—he bounded onto the gang-plank, it bounced him into the air, and light as a feather he came down on it, bounced up again, and landed gracefully on deck. Hey, that's why he gets the big bucks. He comes up to us, breathless, says "I got it," and shows us the paper.

Well, with a build-up like that, from your major star, you'd better hope that it's good. We look at the paper, and beneath a bunch of crossed-off efforts, it says—

"Bring me that horizon!"

Ted and I look at each other.

"That's pretty good," Ted says.

Hell, it was *really* good. We put it together with the previous line and it sounded great, "Let go and haul to run free! Bring me that horizon!"

We took it to Gore. He thought about it for all of half a second, said "That's pretty good. That's really good." Now he even liked the "run free" lead-in, too.

So by midmorning we were rehearsing. The only thing left was the first line, the reference to the crew. Depp gamely tried our first effort, which I think was something like "What are you looking at, you rickets-ridden layabouts! Back to work!" After spitting that out a few times he came over and demanded a better line. He worked through a few, and then Ted came up with "scabrous dogs." So the end line of the movie was finally set:

JACK SPARROW

What are you lookin' at, you scabrous dogs? Back to work! Let go and haul to run free! Bring me that horizon!

As of this writing, I don't know if the movie is good, or if the lines made it in, or even if they work the way they should. But if the film is good, it's fun to think that the final line of the film was written the day it was shot.

I hope it does work.

I hope the movie is great.

Because I've got something pinned above my desk: the scrap of paper Depp was waving as he raced out of the trailer that he wrote the line on.

I kept it, of course.

It has our favorite line in the movie—one we didn't even write!

Darling, the BLACK PEARL HAS ALWAYS Been MINE...
RigHt tHeN, look ALive, MATes!
BRiNg Me tHat HoRizoN...
its FAST !!! xxx

An Amazing Cast of Characters

Johnny Depp
CAPTAIN JACK SPARROW
"...But you *have* heard of me."

To those who have examined the fascinating trajectory of his career, Johnny Depp emerges as more than an actor and more than a movie star. He's nothing less than a supernatural shape-shifter, morphing from one role to another with alarming effectiveness. Perhaps the only commonality in Depp's incredibly widespread choice of roles is his deep compassion for, and understanding of, the outsider, the square peg, the rebel, the one standing just outside the door, either looking for a way in or trying to run in the opposite direction. Which is exactly why Gore Verbinski and Jerry Bruckheimer wanted him to play Captain Jack in Pirates of the Caribbean.

Credit should be given to the viewing habits of Depp's son, Jack, and daughter, Lily-Rose, who had immersed their dad in a world of cartoon characters. He had become impressed by the fact that these characters had virtually no limitations on-screen. In a meeting with his friend Richard "Dick" Cook, Chairman of the Walt Disney Studios, Depp expressed interest in providing the voice for a Disney animated feature. However, an offer that would present him with eminently wilder possibilities was presented when Cook

mentioned that they were hoping to somehow translate the Pirates of the Caribbean attraction into a feature film.

"When we went on a quest to get the first film cast," recalls Bruckheimer, "I figured the way to get an audience to really embrace the movie is to go against the grain. We went after Johnny Depp, a very artistic actor who takes on very quirky projects. He's not out to have a huge audience base, he just wants to make pictures that really excite him creatively and artistically. I visited him during the Cannes Film Festival at his home in France, and he was interested, partially because he now has a couple of kids and wanted to make a film that they could watch and enjoy. He asked us to send him a script, and he committed to the project right after he read it." Depp notes that almost everyone was surprised, including himself, when he immediately responded to Bruckheimer and Verbinski's offer with a quick "I'm in."

> **With Captain Jack Sparrow, it was the perfect opportunity for Johnny to go someplace he hadn't been to before.**
> —GORE VERBINSKI

"Johnny is a virtuoso, the Miles Davis of acting," notes Gore Verbinski. "Johnny always plays against his great looks. He could be a straight-up leading man if he wanted to, but he doesn't have that desire. Johnny is much more into the craft and exploring more avenues for his acting. With Captain Jack Sparrow, it was the perfect opportunity for Johnny to go someplace he hadn't been to before."

Depp's concept of Captain Jack Sparrow started to brew as soon as he read Ted Elliott and Terry Rossio's draft of the screenplay. "What Ted and Terry did in terms of creating a framework for the character was wonderful and amazing," says the actor. "The building blocks were there, and then ideas and images started coming into my mind. I had pretty strong ideas about the kind of ingredients that would go into Jack."

Depp attributes some of Captain Jack's influence to the odiously charming cartoon skunk Pepe Le Pew, but he most tellingly took inspiration from good friend Keith Richards, who remains one of the most potent figures in that most rebellious of all art forms, rock and roll. "They live dangerously," Depp explains. "They're wild and capable of anything, just like pirates." The actor also did some serious

LEFT: The first photo ever taken of Johnny Depp as Jack Sparrow.

thinking about Captain Jack Sparrow in a fairly unusual place for character study: a sauna. "He kind of came to life while I was reading the script in extreme heat, bordering on 200 degrees Fahrenheit," Depp recalls. "The heat was very important to me, the idea of sweltering heat and a guy who's been on the ocean for ten years. I thought that Jack would have perpetual sea legs from being on the water too much, so land becomes really odd and uncomfortable. Jack has been through everything, probably done time in faraway prisons, spent time on deserted islands. So it was the real heat, and the heat that we put into our brain from obsessing or thinking about one thing, combined with the idea that pirates were rock stars of that period."

The truth was, when the first scenes filmed from *The Curse of the Black Pearl* came back to the studio, some executives at the Walt Disney Studios were worried that Depp had been in the heat for a minute too long himself. But

Verbinski and Bruckheimer resolutely stood by their man (as Verbinski points out, "It's our job to make studios nervous."), and Depp himself proffered no instant cures for the studio's concerns about what might be ailing his seemingly bizarre character. "Gore was amazing from day one," Depp confirms. "From the first second that Gore saw me in costume, makeup and wig, he was ecstatic. Gore was unbelievably supportive, even when the upper echelon was telling him that he needed to have a talk with that weirdo and tone him down. Gore just told them, 'I like it. *You* talk to him.' He was very brave, 'ol Gore. We were on the same ride, and enjoying it."

"What Johnny did—and what all great actors do—was to make the character his own," says Bruce Hendricks, Disney's president of physical production and an executive producer of the Pirates films. "During the early days of *The Curse of the Black Pearl* shoot," continues Hendricks,

"somebody said to me, 'What Johnny's doing is either brilliant or completely crazy.' It ended up, naturally, being brilliant." Ted Elliott notes, on behalf of himself and partner Terry Rossio, that "the performance that Johnny gave is not what we imagined—it was *better* than we imagined."

Depp enjoys the character's loopily sunny nature, which lends credence to the notion that he might actually be, "despite all evidence to the contrary," as Captain Jack asserts, a good man. "It seemed to me that Captain Jack was miraculously able to run between the raindrops," says the actor. "I mean, he could entertain both troops, walk across the DMZ, and tell a story to one group, and then go to their enemy and tell them another story, just to stay on the good side of everyone. No matter how bad things get, there was always this bizarre optimism, and maybe a denial. I thought there was something beautiful and poignant about his objective: all he wants is to get the *Black Pearl* back, which represents nothing more than pure freedom to the guy. Of course, he'll take what he can get, whenever the opportunity arises, but the main focus for this guy is to get his ship back at any cost."

On set, Depp projects a warm, gentle kindness and accessibility that mark him as the true Kentucky gentleman and terrifically devoted family man that he is. His natural charisma also illuminated the proceedings with a special light that created a unique atmosphere whenever he was working. Or is that Captain Jack Sparrow's charisma? Because in the middle of a workday, it was impossible for anyone—perhaps himself least of all—to know where Johnny Depp ended and Captain Jack began, and vice versa. For the nearly two-year period between the start of production on *Dead Man's Chest* to the final wrap of *At World's End*, Johnny Depp's smile was the same as Captain Jack's, with the character's trademark

> **What I set out to do was to try and make Captain Jack appeal to little kids as well as the most hardened adult intellectuals.**
>
> —JOHNNY DEPP

For Johnny Depp, the public embrace of Captain Jack Sparrow was a vindication of his typically unorthodox approach to playing a movie pirate. Nonetheless, the modest actor claims that "It is beyond me how such a character has sort of taken root in some people's hearts. It's still shocking to me. I was handed this opportunity to make something of this character, and I had pretty solid ideas about who he was and what he should be like. There were a number of people who thought I was nuts. But I was committed to the guy, and I think that's what happened to me in terms of finding the character. What I set out to do was to try and make Captain Jack appeal to little kids as well as the most hardened adult intellectuals.

"You know, with every character you play, they still reside in there somewhere. It's an occupational hazard, but also a kind of gift in a way. You get to know and to be these guys for a length of time, and you get to like and become close to them. I'm still walking around with all these guys inside of me, like Ed Wood and Raoul Duke, and they show up at odd times. I'm very happy that Captain Jack is in there, too, and I feel safe that he will be with me, always."

gold and silver teeth bonded onto his own. "Jack was a great challenge but ultimately very rewarding for me because he felt good from early on," confirms Depp. "I knew him pretty quickly. You sort of feel like you want to hang with Jack when you watch him."

A wholly original and thrillingly eccentric creation, this ducking, weaving, highly superstitious pirate captain of equally dubious morality and hygiene, slightly ambiguous in his masculinity, desperately trying to believe his own trumped-up self-promotion, became the screen anti-hero for a new century. Against all conventional wisdom, with his long dreadlocks and braided beard adorned with a wild assortment of coins, beads, and baubles, and teeth studded with gold and silver, Captain Jack Sparrow appealed to audiences that ran the gamut in age, gender, and nationality. Depp's performance not only won the 2003 Screen Actors Guild Award plus Academy Award, Golden Globe, and British Academy of Film and Television Arts Award nominations for Best Actor, but his conjuring of Jack Sparrow was also named one of the 100 greatest performances of all time in the May 2006 U.S. edition of *Premiere* magazine.

Tokens of Affection

Captain Jack often helps himself to a souvenir of his romantic encounters. The black and gold ring with three diamonds, Depp decided, was from a Spanish widow. In truth, "The ring with the little skulls I found years ago in a thrift store," he recalls. The other two are the jade "dragon ring" and a large purple stone in a solid gold base that he takes from Tia Dalma. This ring was re-created by propmaster Kris Peck from a 2,400-year-old original that Depp owned until it tragically disappeared during filming.

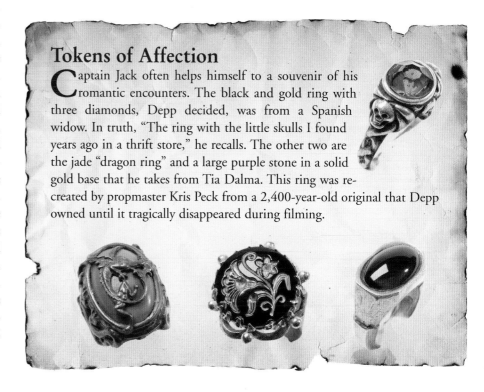

Orlando Bloom
WILL TURNER

"I make a point of avoiding familiarity with pirates."

It's only the most gifted actor who can make the toughest and most challenging roles seem simple, and yet, by the accounts of his director and fellow stars, that's exactly what Orlando Bloom accomplished with his role of Will Turner in Pirates of the Caribbean. On the surface, Will is a classic, dashing young hero, destined to slay the villain, get the girl, and go sailing off into the sunset with nary a nick or scar. But throughout the three films, it's actually Will who undergoes the most drastic and sometimes surprising character trajectories in his literal and figurative journey from innocence to experience.

"Orlando Bloom is just a phenomenon," says Gore Verbinski. "I can't see anyone else in the role of William Turner. He is our D'Artagnan (from *The Three Musketeers*). Deceptively naive, Will grows in complexity throughout the three films."

"Orlando probably had the most difficult role in the films," says Johnny Depp. "At first, Will is a very straight, earnest, uptight character, who in a lot of ways, is the eyes and ears of the audience. There's another purpose to be served in terms of what the audience, or how the audience is going to react, and I thought Orlando pulled it off beautifully."

Jerry Bruckheimer has a knack for discovering young talent before the rest of the world catches on. He cast Bloom as an ill-fated young U.S. Ranger in *Black Hawk Down* before The Lord of the Rings trilogy, which propelled Bloom to worldwide superstardom, was released. "I thought he was a brilliant young actor," Bruckheimer recalls, "and I thought his time would come. I talked to Orlando about playing Will Turner when we were making *Black Hawk Down*, and he expressed interest. Then *The Fellowship of the Ring* hit, and we were lucky to grab him as all of the frenzy began to happen."

From the get-go, Bloom had always perceived that Pirates was, to a large extent, Will Turner's coming-of-age story, and was attracted by the challenge of playing a character who would wind up in a very different place from where he started. It's not every day that one is asked to play an eighteenth century blacksmith who despises pirates, only to become one himself. "Will is quite straightlaced in the beginning, but he really does develop through the course of the three movies," notes the actor. "If you imagine him in one of those corsets that Keira wears as Elizabeth, which I admit is a pretty funny thought, then in the beginning of the first film it's very tight, everything is tense, and Will can hardly breathe.

As you move through the films, Will starts to untie the laces, breathes a little more, becomes more of a real and understanding person. But Gore always reminded me not to forget who Will was in the beginning—a slightly nervous, dorky blacksmith, just a boy in love with a girl well above his station."

By the finale of *The Curse of the Black Pearl*, Will was a swashbuckling hero in the classic tradition, but had also, by helping to save Captain Jack from the gallows, become an outlaw. The harsh truth about his father's piracy leads Will on an inexorable path to self-discovery and a deeply surprising denouement to his story.

"When we started talking about the prospect of doing *Dead Man's Chest* and *At World's End*," says Bloom, "I was keen to try and have some element of a real character development, which obviously they were already thinking of. I wanted Will to be less the kind of earnest, upright young guy and see a darker side to his character, within the bounds of the story. Will's real journey throughout the second and third movies is his concern for his father, Bootstrap Bill, and his growing desperation to rescue his father from the fate he's been destined to live, which is at the bottom of the ocean on the *Flying Dutchman* serving Davy Jones as one of his crew.

63

Davy Jones's world, so Will sees that relationship disappearing before his eyes. What's fantastic about the third film is that the character development that begins in *Dead Man's Chest* continues to grow and build, and the momentum pulls you forward. At the end of the second movie, you really want to see where the story's going."

Physically fearless, Bloom—who once broke his back while indulging in horseplay with a group of friends—insisted on doing his own stunts whenever feasible, completely at home whilst thirty-five feet aloft on a ship's mast, and he gloried in swordplay. Says Pirates stunt coordinator George Marshall Ruge, who also worked with the actor on all three The Lord of the Rings films, "In terms of the physical action, Orlando was probably the most willing and enthusiastic. Orly has a wonderful sense about himself and the characters he plays, and that translated to a very 'can do' approach to the physical action. Plus, he's had a lot of experience in the period/action genre."

Bloom himself could not have been happier or more grateful to have come upon a role like Will Turner, which he calls "a great gig."

"To be honest, it's every boy's dream to be doing this kind of swashbuckling pirate movie. I feel like I'm living many dreams all at the same time, whether it's getting to kiss the beautiful girl, swinging from ropes, sliding down sails, or rolling down mountaintops in bone cages. The actual work that goes into it is really difficult, though it's made to look easy on camera, but it's so much fun doing it. Thanks to Gore and everyone on set, there's a real feeling of high-flying. I can't imagine that movies will ever be done like this again. I think we all feel very lucky to be involved."

But Will also wants to maintain his relationship with Elizabeth, and he's torn between those two objectives. It poses an interesting conundrum for Will, and hopefully, for the audience as well.

"In *Dead Man's Chest*, Will can't really understand the intentions of Captain Jack and Elizabeth," continues Bloom. "Elizabeth has her objectives, which conflict with Will's to some extent. And she forms a relationship with Jack that feels questionable to Will, but he really doesn't know the ins and outs of it. He's trying to put the pieces of the puzzle together without really knowing what those pieces are. So he jumps to conclusions that create friction between him and Elizabeth. And his father is vanishing more and more into

Keira Knightley
ELIZABETH SWANN
"I think it would be rather exciting to meet a pirate."

On *The Curse of the Black Pearl*, Keira Knightley was thrilled with her role of Elizabeth Swann, except for one tragic omission: she continually begged for, but never received, a sword in her hand. So on *Dead Man's Chest*, the filmmakers took pity on her, and gave her two—one for each hand—which she then wielded with deadly accuracy. "On the first film, I kept saying 'I'm in a pirate movie, I want to swordfight,'" says Knightley. "And they wouldn't give it to me. I fought with candlesticks and long, golden Aztec poles, even one of those heating bed-pan things, but nobody gave me a sword. I was completely ignored in the whole fencing area. So in *Dead Man's Chest* and *At World's End*, I have many sword fights, and two swords as well, so I'm very happy now."

Keira Knightley was a mere seventeen years old when she was cast by Gore Verbinski and Jerry Bruckheimer in *Pirates of the Caribbean: The Curse of the Black Pearl*, and hadn't yet been discovered by international audiences in her break-through movie, *Bend It Like Beckham*. "My agent called me while I was looking at gossip magazines in a bookstore in London," Knightley recalls, "and told me to meet with the casting people in London. I turned up for the audition about half an hour late, dripping with sweat, because it was a really odd, warm day in London, which doesn't normally happen. I read a quick scene that was videotaped and thought I did horrifically, but the next day they rang up and asked me go to Los Angeles to meet with Gore. That was my first time in Los Angeles, a very Hollywood experience. Then they told me to fly to New York to meet Jerry."

For the filmmakers, it was a natural decision. "There was an innocence and beauty about her," recalls Bruckheimer, "but I think you hire an actress like Keira because of her ability. The fact that she's gorgeous helps, but she's such a talented performer, you believe her, and that's the key." Adds Gore Verbinski, "Not knowing anything about Keira except for her coming in and reading, we were 'Yeah, let's roll the dice with her,' and then being completely surprised by the depth of her talent."

During the filming of *Dead Man's Chest*, Terry Rossio noted, "If there's a scene being shot with Keira in it, you know it's going to work. And you look forward to those scenes." Adds Ted Elliott, "There is some very tricky stuff that goes on in these stories, and some things that I think genuinely surprise and challenge the audience. And I'm not sure that if we didn't have Keira playing Elizabeth we would have tried that. But we always feel very confident. We've got Keira. Don't worry. It'll work."

"The great thing about Elizabeth Swann," says Knightley about her character, "is that she has this obsession with pirates that you see from the first scene and she's romanticized the entire thing. So it's an interesting transition going from the romance of it to where the reality hits, which turns out to be cutthroat with lots of scars and tattoos, and very dirty. I think at first she's starstruck at meeting the infamous Jack Sparrow, but then he puts a gun to her head. It's understandable that he wants to escape, but as far as Elizabeth is concerned, it's not exactly gratitude for saving someone's life.

"I think the moment she's captured by Barbossa, although it's dreadful and scary, it's actually a huge moment of freedom. The adventurous spirit in her is really awakened, and now she's in her element. Elizabeth is a little pirate herself," adds Knightley. "Aren't we all?"

> **You hire an actress like Keira because of her ability. The fact that she's gorgeous helps, but she's such a talented performer, you believe her, and that's the key.**
>
> —JERRY BRUCKHEIMER

For the second and third Pirates films, Knightley experienced a new acting challenge. "I've never played the same character twice. I thought I wouldn't be able to change anything from the way I played her before, but Elizabeth gets quite a bit darker. It's been roughly two years between the first and second films, and she's grown up in those two years.

"She was on the brink of being married," Knightley continues, "which all falls flat. This adds some very nice undertones as far as her relationships go—her relationship with Will is falling apart and her relationship with Jack grows into something rather interesting. So there were a lot of new bits within her that I could grab on to."

"Keira is a extraordinary actress," says Bruckheimer, "and we saw that when we cast her in the first Pirates movie at the age of seventeen. For *Dead Man's Chest*, she's almost twenty-one. You can see how she's matured, so we used that to our advantage. The character's matured. The skills that Keira had in the first movie have been heightened through the amount of work that she's done. She's a very young girl with the amazing gift of being not only beautiful, but a terrific actress."

Like so many others, Knightley was pleasantly surprised to discover that their venture was a phenomenal success. "Nobody had made a successful pirate movie in a long time, and we thought, this is crazy, but the movie is interesting and looks great. Actually, how much people loved *The Curse of the Black Pearl* was a real surprise. And I think a lot of that had to do, obviously, with Gore Verbinski, who is fantastic, and also with what Johnny did with the character. His portrayal of Jack Sparrow brought the movie into a whole new world."

But so did Knightley. Like the actress herself, Elizabeth Swann is an appealing blend of brains and beauty, steel and softness, femininity and tomboyishness co-existing side-by-side, even merging, without the one canceling out the other. Knightley, who has bucketloads of spirit, talent, and confidence without an ounce of arrogance, knew the character of Elizabeth Swann from the starting line. "Elizabeth Swann is a twenty-first century girl stuck in an eighteenth-century world. She's really modern, really cool, strong and very independent, and kicks ass."

Geoffrey Rush
CAPTAIN BARBOSSA

"You'd best start believing in ghost stories, Miss Turner. You're in one."

Rarely has such a dastardly scoundrel been so truly beloved as the gloriously wicked Captain Barbossa, portrayed by the versatile Geoffrey Rush. If there are any doubts, just witness the roars of approval that greet Barbossa's surprise appearance at the last seconds of *Dead Man's Chest*—finally slaking his appetite by lustily chomping on a sweet, juicy apple, his (undead) pet monkey on his shoulder.

That such a blackguard could become so popular is entirely due to the unbridled gusto and brio with which Rush tore into his role of Barbossa, not to mention the humanity of a man, however unsavory, who suffered in the first film from the curse of being neither dead nor fully alive. "It's all because of the apples," notes the Academy Award-winning actor. "Barbossa just wanted to taste something as simple as the sweetness of an apple."

"Barbossa's the quintessential villain," says director Gore Verbinski. "Geoffrey Rush was able to play and celebrate the two-dimensional aspects of a character like this, yet play the depth all the way in terms of the needs and wants of the character who just wants to taste food again."

For *The Curse of the Black Pearl*, the thoughtful actor developed an elaborate backstory for Barbossa to explain who and what he is. "Pirates of that age tended to come from England's West Country, and I decided that Barbossa's mother was Irish," says Rush, who perfected the pirate's delicious accent, at once musical and terrifying, with dialect coach Barbara Berkery. "I put this story together that when he was about thirteen, Barbossa ran away to sea because he came from a background of poverty. And he would have been on ships where he would have seen very grand cabins and the captains living in spacious and elegant quarters. And he thought, that's where I want to be.

"Barbossa may have had very earnest desires to be a man of the sea, but realized pretty quickly that you could actually get a lot more if you broke the rules, lied to people, and killed a few in the process. So Barbossa became greedy, with horrible social pretensions. And," he adds, "you don't get to be in Barbossa's position of power by being a fool. He's cunning, wily, and manipulative. I actually think he's quite smart, it's probably why he's survived. He's a horrible liar, and he pretends to be a gentleman of the sea, but he's a dirty, old, cunning rogue."

And a crack swordsman. "And a nasty one," Rush confirms. "He didn't go to finishing school with an épée, he just had a sword on his belt and learned how to skewer people and survive. When he pulls his sword out, even big guys cower away." During the training, Geoffrey developed what he calls "cutlass elbow." "I did a lot of work on the sword training, because I figured if you don't believe he's good at it, then you don't believe *in* it."

Rush was delighted with all of the accoutrements that converted him into a suitably gnarled, scarred, scarifying sea dog, including Ve Neill's makeup and Martin Samuel's wig, as well as Penny Rose's costume. "Barbossa's costume is almost operatic in its intensity, somehow managing to look grimy, dangerous, foul, ugly, and thrilling, but still somehow looking as though we are in a classic pirates story for children," says Rush.

The actor was quite pleased to bring Barbossa back to life in *Dead Man's Chest*, particularly since he sees the films as considerably more than just popcorn entertainment, especially for younger viewers. "I've always felt that the film has got a great nineteenth century Dickensian sort of dimension to it, where you're not following just one or two stories," says Rush. "The payoffs become even richer in *At World's End* when even more characters are introduced.

"With Barbossa's return," he continues, "you have a complex series of adventures. In *At World's End*, these pirates have had their Golden Age of being free spirits, where they're not beholden to any government or national boundaries. And there is a definite awareness among them that this world is changing, becoming a much more mercantile environment. With characters like Captain Jack and Barbossa, there's a sort of reluctant, mutual admiration society because they both realize that they're survivors.

"When Barbossa re-emerges after being absent in the second film, he actually comes back as a kind of politician and that was great for me because I didn't have to play the same flavors or work off the same dramatic palette as in the first film. My job now is to make sure that the romantic heritage of the pirates being the vagabond brotherhood at sea maintains its identity against this ruthless corporate world. So he's become an arch manipulator, which plays well with Barbossa's qualities of betraying and forcing people to do things they don't particularly want to do."

Rush happily compliments his simian partner. "She was fantastic, pretending to be a boy monkey—she was really *acting*," he says with a laugh. "Though I was trained to have no relationship with her, I could feel her little head and smell her little monkey breath. Occasionally she would start to search for things in my wig, but she would be told not to do that because it meant we were getting on too well. The monkey always worked through the trainer."

Perhaps it takes someone with Geoffrey Rush's range of experience in serious film and theater to truly understand much of what lies at the heart of the Pirates story. "One can only hope," says the actor with a smile, "that there are some—but not too many—meaningful college essays that are going to be written about the political semiotics and philosophical underpinnings of Pirates of the Caribbean. And they will be a joy to read, and quite amusing at the same time."

Bill Nighy
DAVY JONES
"Life is cruel. Why should the afterlife be any different?"

After a thirty-year career as one of the finest character actors that Great Britain has offered to the rest of the world, one might have thought that Bill Nighy had played it all, seen it all, and done it all. "But now, I'm probably the only man in the world who's been required to play the organ with an imaginary beard comprised of octopus tentacles," the gentlemanly Nighy says with more than a touch of his typical self-deprecating wit.

Gore Verbinski selected the extraordinarily versatile Nighy to portray Davy Jones, knowing that he would find the humanity beneath the beastly veneer of one no longer human but not a complete monster, so torn by love that the emotional pain has caused him to literally rip his heart from his body. Nighy's genius was to play the character large enough to transcend Davy Jones's extraordinary appearance, yet subtle enough to penetrate the character's soul, and the audience's as well.

"Davy Jones is a deeply damaged and isolated individual," the award-winning actor explains. "He's wounded so deeply that he determines that he will live a kind of semi-life, a kind of half death/half life, as long as it means he doesn't have to feel anything anymore. So he's torn out the center of all feeling—his heart—and locked it in a special chest. He also has control of a 'pet,' which is the Kraken, a sea monster the likes of which you've never seen before—entirely malevolent, evil, and powerful beyond expression. If you possess Davy Jones's

heart, you control not only him, but the Kraken as well, which in effect gives you control of the oceans."

The question could be posed—is Davy Jones a hero or a villain? "Sure he's misunderstood and he's had a few troubles in his past," says Nighy, "but I wouldn't put him up there with the evil people. . . . No, he's evil," he recounts. "He is currently operating as a very, very evil force in the world. Because he hurts so bad, he figures, why shouldn't the rest of the world? He has suffered, in his view, in a way that few people suffer. So he sees no reason why anyone else should not suffer similarly."

Nighy's primary challenge would be that, because of Jones's astonishing physical appearance, as imagined by Gore Verbinski, conceptual consultant James Ward Byrkit, and conceptual artist Mark "Crash" McCreery, he would be required to wear not a costume but a "motion-capture suit." The outfit, which Nighy humorously describes as resembling "deeply attractive" gray pajamas and a matching cap, were lined with reference marks that Industrial Light & Magic's computer wizards, including visual effects supervisor John Knoll, would use to execute his appearance. Says Jerry Bruckheimer, "Bill had to work under a lot of constraints technically, but did it with such ease and in such a way that he created a real character. That's a very difficult thing to do, and when you see his performance as Davy Jones you realize just how brilliantly Bill pulled it off."

"In the beginning," says Nighy, "there was discussion of working the computer imagery off of an existing prosthetic that I would have worn, but I'm grateful that we didn't do that because it proved not to be necessary. Also, in the kind of heat in which we were filming in the Caribbean, I'm really, *really* grateful not to have had to wear a prosthetic!"

"Every now and then," the actor said in an interview with *dreamwatch* magazine, "Gore would have to say, 'Remember you have a squid growing out of your chin.' The temptation is to get into people's faces."

Nighy himself was absolutely game to take the role on. "To play a character who is physically embellished by computer wizardry, you still use your imagination as an actor," he explains. "The same things are required of you, generally speaking. There's a leap of faith involved. And you're also affected by the fact that you're playing a character that's extraordinary, a creature beyond human. You feel you have to inhabit that in a way that you perhaps wouldn't if you were playing naturalistically. So there's a spin on it that perhaps would not otherwise be there." The character's many levels are almost as multi-layered as the *Flying Dutchman*'s strata of encrustation. "And you have to play the man he once was," Nighy explained in *Empire* magazine. "It's difficult to conceive of playing a bloomin' squid."

ABOVE: The first rendering of Davy Jones, sketched in the middle of the night by conceptual consultant James Ward Byrkit during one of his "spitball sessions" with Gore Verbinski; RIGHT: Davy Jones finds his octopod form in this Crash McCreery illustration.

Stellan Skarsgård
"BOOTSTRAP BILL" TURNER
"Once you've sworn an oath to the *Dutchman,* there's no leaving it."

I n *Pirates of the Caribbean: Dead Man's Chest* and *At World's End,* Stellan Skarsgård portrays the character responsible for Will Turner's presence in the Caribbean. After learning that his father toils in servitude to Davy Jones and the *Flying Dutchman,* losing the last vestiges of his humanity in the process, Will vows to set him free. Skarsgård brought a great sense of both dignity and melancholy to Bootstrap Bill, which deepens the inherent father-son tragedy.

"Stellan is an astonishingly talented actor," notes Jerry Bruckheimer. "Johnny and Orlando both wanted to work with him. I had the great fortune to work with Stellan on *King Arthur,* and he created a wonderful character for us in that film. And he does it all over again with Bootstrap Bill. Stellan shaped this compassionate, interesting character who's slowly going mad. It's a very subtle performance."

Like Bill Nighy, Skarsgård is an actor strong enough to transcend the physical boundaries of the role. When he was originally approached for the part, Skarsgård was under the impression that he might be spared the lengthy daily ritual in the makeup trailer. "When I was first contacted, I saw sketches of Bootstrap Bill in six different stages," he explains, "so I was very much aware of what he would look like. But I thought it would mostly be CGI." Initial makeup tests proved to look much better than anticipated, and so it was decided that Bootstrap Bill's slow transformation worked better with prosthetics than with computer-generated enhancements. This would require the actor to spend upwards of four-and-a-half hours a day in the makeup chair. "I can blame it all on Ve Neill and Joel Harlow," Skarsgård confirms, "who created fabulous makeup designs that worked better for the progression of the character.

"It's very soft," the actor continues, "and you can do any expression with it. I'm very happy about it, because I don't feel that I am deprived of my possibilities in realizing the character."

Skarsgård's interest in portraying Bootstrap Bill was heightened by his initial meetings with Gore Verbinski. "The kinds of discussions I had with Gore made me believe in him very much as a sensitive and intelligent person that I could enjoy working with," he recalls.

Skarsgård, who has worked with some of the most rigorously artistic directors in Europe, found that Gore Verbinski had much in common with those filmmakers. "Gore is an auteur, as we say in Europe, because he puts his own personal stamp on the film," explains the actor. "He either keeps away from the cliches, or he uses the cliches and makes fun of them. That gives a sort of unique life to what he's doing, I think. And Gore is interested in actors, which you could see in the first Pirates film. There was a lot of space for actors to bloom and expand within scenes. And it also has to do with the way characters are portrayed. They're not just one-dimensional. It's a very liberal atmosphere on set. You can come up with any suggestion you want or try a second take that is very different from the first. It's not about repetition, but about searching for expressions in every scene that bring the story to life and make the characters interesting.

"And there's not only one solution to everything— there are a million solutions that are all right. It's all about playing around to see what you can squeeze out of a scene. And see if it *rocks.*"

Chow Yun-Fat
CAPTAIN SAO FENG
"It seems the only way a pirate can turn a profit anymore is by betraying other pirates."

The United States and Europe have movie stars. Asia, on the other hand, has demigods who happen to star in movies. It's difficult for many to make this cultural leap and understand the exalted position that actors such as Chow Yun-Fat hold in their own worlds. The Hong Kong–born star is the most popular actor in Asia, which means that in sheer numbers, he's one of the most popular actors in the world. It's that simple.

And that's the way it's been for the past twenty years, since Chow's starring role in John Woo's *A Better Tomorrow* made cinema history, breaking box-office records in every East and Southeast Asian country in which it opened. The film made Chow (who, like most East Asians, goes by his family name first and given name second) a superstar, a position he's held ever since. Mention his name, and one adjective leaps to mind: charisma. And it was exactly that quality which made Chow Yun-Fat a perfect choice to portray Captain Sao Feng, the majestic, terrifying, and curiously romantic Pirate Lord of Singapore in *At World's End*.

"I thought the first Pirates of the Caribbean film was marvelous," says the actor. "I just loved it. So having a chance to work on the third film was just like a little child walking in a dream." Chow Yun-Fat has made relatively few English-language films, but he was keen to appear in the third installment for Jerry Bruckheimer and Gore Verbinski. "This performance in the third Pirates film is totally different from anything else I've done, I think."

It certainly *looks* different from anything else Chow Yun-Fat has done. The handsome actor underwent a daily three-hour makeup and hair session to convert him into a suitably gnarly, bald, tattooed, rotten-toothed, scarred vision of Asian piracy, rendering him virtually unrecognizable. "No big deal," Chow comments about the ritual. "I got used to it."

Considering the intensity of many of his on-screen performances, Chow constantly impressed and delighted his fellow actors and crew members with his irrepressibly joyful and affectionate nature, given to wide smiles, impromptu hugs, and a general air of absolute delight in being on set, both in Los Angeles and Grand Bahama Island. "Yun-Fat gave the entire company a new lease on life when he came on," recalls Gore Verbinski. "There's nothing he wouldn't do. He would even help the grips push equipment around if he could." Even the magnificent costume designed by Penny

Rose, which weighed more than twenty pounds, had little effect on his infectious optimism. "I'm a tough guy, I can handle it," he says with a grin.

Yun-Fat relishes the role of the duplicitous but noble captain. "I'm a pirate. I can do whatever I want. But the pirate world is very tricky. Everyone's betraying each other. It's a very mysterious and complicated situation. But I like it."

Kevin R. McNally
JOSHAMEE GIBBS

Joshamee Gibbs is a staunch ally of Captain Jack Sparrow and a sailor's sailor. A Royal Navy man turned pirate (as so many did in historical reality), he is a teller of tales both tall and short, with an epicurean taste for rum and all other manner of consciousness-altering beverages. He's also brave, bold, and loyal, all of which, among pirates, are attributes in rather short commodity.

A well-known actor in his native Britain, Kevin R. McNally made his feature film debut in the James Bond adventure *The Spy Who Loved Me*, and has never stopped working since on screen, television, and stage. And as such, he was determined to properly prepare for his role. "If Gibbs isn't out at sea, then he's drinking with the pigs, so the research was interesting," McNally says jokingly. "I have a very crusty accent as Gibbs, which I sort of based on Robert Newton in *Treasure Island* and Robert Shaw as Quint from *Jaws*, and I've come up with a hybrid of my own." Gibbs's makeup and wardrobe also helped contribute to McNally's rich characterization, although, with the first film, "I had a terrible decision to make in the beginning—should I have people gluing hair to my face every day but still look normal in real life, or look like a hillbilly for a year? I went for the real thing, which made filming decidedly easier, though I returned to England with the most beautiful tan—apart from two white stripes down the sides of my face!"

For the second and third Pirates films, McNally was

challenged by the new direction the story took, especially in the action sequences. "I'm doing quite a lot of my own stunts, and I would like to say that's because I'm very brave . . . but that isn't it. I really like [assistant stunt coordinator and double] Dan Barringer, but Gore doesn't think that Dan and I look similar enough." After filming the Bone Cage falling over the cliff in *Dead Man's Chest* using Barringer, it was realized that "what they really needed was my face," McNally recalls. "So I thought they'd put me in front of a blue screen, shoot my face, and matte it in later. But no, what they did was strap me into the cage with a camera and then threw me over a cliff—well, really a small hill. The acting's really good . . . I'm acting really scared!

"*Dead Man's Chest* was definitely much more physically exerting," McNally admits. "In the first film, Gibbs was a drunk and it wasn't until the end of the film, when there were about five of us facing eighty invincible pirates, that Gibbs had to pick up a sword and start fighting. And now, he's rather proved himself so he's always picking up a sword, which is a very bad character move for me. I liked it when I just had to lie around with pigs."

McNally happily gives credit to the team of filmmakers for the rich and inspiring environment he's been able to work in for the course of the three films. "If you're in a big action picture, I suppose you would worry that you'd get lost in it all. But the great thing about Ted and Terry's writing and Gore's direction is that what they're most interested in are the characters. So there are massive scenes and massive sets around us, but the real meat of the film is when we all get down, talk, plan, and plot, and just be pirates."

Jonathan Pryce
GOVERNOR WEATHERBY SWANN

One of the most respected and honored stage and screen actors in the English-speaking world, Jonathan Pryce jokingly says that, when offered the role of Governor Weatherby Swann, Elizabeth's loving if somewhat befuddled father, he was most enticed by the locations. "What I liked most about the character was that he worked in Los Angeles, and also in the Caribbean. But it really *was* attractive to play. There was a lot of wit that could be brought to the role, although," he teases, "the sad thing about playing this role is that I'm playing him deadly serious. It's rather disturbing that everyone finds him rather funny—I must find out where I've gone wrong."

Having missed the premieres of the first film because of his schedule, Pryce finally bought himself a ticket in London, "and could barely get a seat, since the cinema was packed. It was a wonderful experience seeing the film with a real audience, hearing them laughing and watching the screen in amazement. It was very gratifying to be in a commercial film that audiences, young and old, responded to so well.

"I never expected to be back," Pryce admits, when asked about returning to the role in both *Dead Man's Chest* and *At World's End*. "but it's been good for me because there's a development of the character through to what possibly will be his ultimate demise and his ultimate resurrection. Things have changed for Swann—the power is being taken from him. The East India Trading Company and this horrible little

person called Lord Cutler Beckett have come in and taken over everything. The nearest modern analogy is that Beckett is a corporate business coming in to take over the small businesses, or in this case, the small governorship that has been a comfortable living for Governor Swann. It's like the globalization of society. I think it's very interesting that an adventure film has underlying modern credibility.

"So," Pryce continues, "Swann has to make a choice whether or not to work with these guys and give them a credible face. He will still be governor, but rather than being answerable immediately to the crown in England, he'll be working for the corporation." But Swann's first and foremost concern is Elizabeth. "That's why he gives in. To hopefully save his daughter."

Pryce was impressed with the authenticity of the many sets and locations, as well as the scale of the moviemaking. "It supports everything you do. The scene in Cutler Beckett's office [where Swann submits to trading his authority in an effort to save Elizabeth] is essentially three characters in an office. Normally that would be a fairly intimate scene. Then you look out the window and there's a whole world going on outside. Ships are being loaded. People are moving. Bananas are going up and down the gangplank. It's all happening over my shoulder. A lot of films would do that on CGI. This was a great approach to filmmaking," he reflects. "It's a great mix of old-fashioned swashbuckling filmmaking and modern technology."

As with many movie period pieces, costume and hair design contribute to the characterization, although Pryce confesses that he thoroughly enjoyed the scenes where he wasn't required to wear the big wig. "Given the heat, that was a blessing. And you disappear under the thing. But it was also very interesting to act as *me* for a bit."

Jack Davenport
JAMES NORRINGTON
"So, this is where your heart truly lies then?"

It's debatable as to which character in the Pirates of the Caribbean films goes through the greatest story arc, but James Norrington would give anyone a good run for their money. From the stiff-upper-lip British naval officer courting Elizabeth Swann in the first film, to the pathetic, ass-over-teakettle drunk re-introduced in a raucous Tortuga tavern in the second film, to the professionally redeemed but morally compromised accomplice of Lord Cutler Beckett in the third, the complex personage of Norrington allows the man who portrays him in all his myriad facets—Jack Davenport—to give full range to his considerable thespian talents.

Davenport came into the world with as fine a pedigree an actor can have as the son of noted actress Maria Aitken and the great Nigel Davenport, who starred with Anthony Quinn and James Coburn in Alexander Mackendrick's *A High Wind in Jamaica,* perhaps the last really fine pirate movie before the genre hit the skids.

That thought was very much on Davenport's mind when he first met with Gore Verbinski about playing the role of Norrington. "My first reaction when I read the script of the first movie was echoed by something that Gore initially said to me: when was the last time I saw a decent pirate movie? I was intrigued by that as well as who else was in the cast. It seemed incredible to me that such a high genre piece was being made, and on such a huge scale." Davenport was also intrigued by the layers of Norrington's character as written by Ted Elliott and Terry Rossio in their draft of the script. "I liked that he wasn't a too-oft seen English villain. I didn't

have to spend the entire film standing in the prow of a boat snarling about pirates getting away. Norrington is basically the scourge of piracy in the eastern Caribbean at the start. If you're a pirate and you see me coming, you'd be scared. I suppose that Norrington's job is to bring light where there is dark, and air freshener to where pirates have recently vacated. Norrington's feelings toward pirates is that they're basically scum. They dress badly, they rob, they cheat, they have very poor personal hygiene. Like any upstanding member of the British military in the eighteenth century, Norrington frowns on that kind of unethical behavior and looks forward to pounding more colonials into the dust with his larger weaponry.

"When the second film begins," Davenport continues, "Norrington has lost big time on all fronts. He lost his girl, lost criminals from the jail—he was humiliated in every way. But hopefully you got a sense of him making mature decisions at a difficult time. The thing that always interested me about the role is that you have this character who is a leader of men in a very public role. And at the end of the first movie, Norrington is in a situation in which, in a very public arena, he's had to deal with things that are incredibly private."

On a sweltering Dominica day, Davenport admitted that he wasn't quite expecting to reprise his role in the second and third films. "To be perfectly honest, I didn't think I stood a prayer of coming back, in the sense that you have to consider how your character serves the story, and one could argue that Norrington totally served his function in a narrative sense because he's kind of the secondary bad guy in the first film. It would be feasible to move the story on and leave Norrington behind, but thankfully, they didn't do that. So here I am, sweating like a pig."

"To be honest with you," says Jerry Bruckheimer, "Jack Davenport is such a superb actor that we wanted him to be back with the party because he's fun to work with and created a memorable character. He really embellishes the movie, so he became an even more major player in both *Dead Man's Chest* and *At World's End*."

At the Pirates workplace, Davenport's veddy British humor—drier than a gin and tonic in a West End pub—was an unending source of amusement for his colleagues, particularly the other stars. "If you can think of the set as a playground," says Keira Knightley, "and you've got the person who can transcend all the different cliques and make everybody laugh, it's Jack Davenport. He is one of the funniest men I have ever met in my entire life. He will always bring a smile to everybody's face, it doesn't matter what's going on, how hard the day is—if you go to see Jack, you'll brighten up. Jack is a fantastic actor and a joy to be around."

Giles New & Angus Barnett
MURTOGG & MULLROY

Giles New (Murtogg, left) and Angus Barnett (Mullroy, right) became fast friends on set, which only helped their on-screen chemistry. "The earnestness of the two characters was very appealing," notes Barnett. "Murtogg and Mullroy would like to think that they're the best guards in the Royal Marines, but actually they're disastrous. If you just saw them alone, you'd wonder how the British ever got an empire. Or maybe that's how we lost it." Adds Giles New, "Since I had never been in a film before *The Curse of the Black Pearl*, I was kind of scared and confused most of the time on set, but I figured that it would be all right because it was right for Murtogg."

New's introduction to filming in Hollywood was, in fact, the last scene in the film, where Jack Sparrow is rescued from a hanging. "In fact, my first shot in my first film ever was a parrot repeatedly relieving himself on my face. The props guy who was doing it was an amazingly accurate shot, and got me in the eye every time. Well, they always say 'Hire the best.'"

Lee Arenberg & Mackenzie Crook
PINTEL & RAGETTI

True to their roles, British native Mackenzie Crook (Ragetti, left) and U.S.-born Lee Arenberg (Pintel, right) genuinely hit it off during the filming of the first Pirates film, inseparable offscreen as well as on. "We sort of stuck together like some sort of eighteenth-century piratical Laurel and Hardy," notes Arenberg. "I always say that the luckiest thing that happened to me is that they couldn't find a short, bald, and crazy guy in London who was the right match for Mackenzie. So they had an audition for short, bald, and crazy guys in Hollywood, and that was a little bit of kismet for me."

Notes Crook, "Pintel and Ragetti are pirates who, like most pirates, can swing either good or bad depending on who's paying the best fee. They're the classic bumbling double act. I'm the complete idiot who will do anything he's told, whereas Lee, as Pintel, is the brains behind the operation, but 'brains' is relative because he hasn't got any either."

"Pintel and Ragetti are marvelous characters to begin with," says Jerry Bruckheimer, "but Lee and Mackenzie did a brilliant job of taking something that was on the page and amping it to the nth degree."

Fortunately, Pintel and Ragetti had the foresight to stick their hands up and surrender at the end of the first movie. "We were smiling then," Crook says, "because we knew we were making the sequel, and all the other guys fooling around on deck didn't!"

"The coolest thing now," adds Arenberg, "is that we're on Jack Sparrow's side. Not only is it cool to work with Johnny, but the Captain Jack character obviously has the best dental plan."

It's a shame the same can't be said about having a vision plan. Ragetti's eye has become a major star unto itself, and Crook reveals that he didn't hear that it was necessary for the character until after he was cast in the part. "Well, I have gotten used to it. It is a bit uncomfortable, but it's also great for the character. I don't feel like Ragetti unless I have this huge wooden eye, which is actually a soft and a hard contact lens sandwiched on top of each other. I can't see out of it when I've got the soft one in, so with no depth perception, I'm always fumbling around, trying to find out how far things are away from me."

Regardless of the difficulties of the filmmaking—including chasing after a runaway eye, sword fighting in a dress, or hanging right-side-up on an upside-down ship—this popular duo are extremely happy with how things have worked out. Pirates of the Caribbean has "tapped into the romantic spirit," notes Arenberg. "The idea of a pirate being a free spirit in a world that's now constricting around you—that's why we love Jack Sparrow. You can't quite catch him, he's slippery. He's a free spirit, and that's what Pintel and Ragetti are, too. We're just not as classy about it."

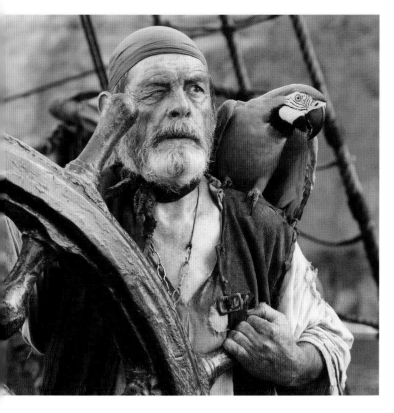

David Bailie
COTTON

I struggled hard to find a background for Cotton, why he had his tongue cut out," confesses David Bailie, the South African–born, England-trained actor who portrays the mute Cotton. "During our first interview, Gore Verbinski suggested I should puzzle it out." Bailie came up with something while shooting the first film that seemed to be logical, but never really tied into the story for him. When he was brought back to film *Dead Man's Chest*, he realized the answer could be as apparent as the tip of his tongue—if he had one. "Now I think the Pelegostos did it. I still haven't figured out how Cotton trained the parrot to speak for him, though.

"I went into a state of bliss when I heard they wanted me back for the second and third movies," Bailie says. "I'm in my mid-sixties, and not many actors can round off their careers doing three major movies and all that that implies."

Martin Klebba
MARTY

My character was originally named Dirk, but somebody—I think it was Gore Verbinski—preferred to use my real name instead," says Martin Klebba. "Marty is from the island of Tortuga, and obviously he's a short-statured guy, but the one thing about pirates is that they didn't discriminate against anybody. They'll treat you as an equal as long as you pull your own weight. Marty is just like anyone else on the *Black Pearl*. As long as he's being paid, it's all good but, like the others, Marty doesn't really have an allegiance to anybody but himself."

In addition to his acting, Marty Klebba is also a professional stuntman and, as such, has performed his own stunts on set. "It makes the story that much more real when you see the actual actor doing it. And I love doing them."

Once in costume and makeup, Marty asserts, "I change. Once you get into it, it's like—boom!—I'm not Marty anymore, I'm *Marty*. Well, that doesn't make any sense, but I'm totally different when I'm in character. Marty's determined to get to where he wants to go through life and be respected. And he's enjoying the opportunity to work with one of the greatest pirates." As to the keys around his neck, costume designer Penny Rose "decided that before I was a pirate, I was quite a womanizer, so these actually represent the keys to women's hearts."

Tom Hollander
LORD CUTLER BECKETT

"There's something to knowing the exact shape of the world and man's place in it. Don't you agree?"

One of the two primary villains of *Dead Man's Chest* and *At World's End*—perhaps even more villainous than Davy Jones—is the cold, calculating, and utterly ruthless Lord Cutler Beckett. Invited to inhabit this dastardly soul was Tom Hollander, who so brilliantly portrayed Mister Collins, the diminutive and hapless suitor of

Keira Knightley's Elizabeth Bennet in 2006's *Pride & Prejudice*. Hollander was attracted to playing Beckett because, like the other characters developed for both the first and second films, he was multidimensional.

"Soft glove, hard fist," notes Tom Hollander of his character. "On the outside, he's very arrogant and charming, but the inside is incredibly hard." Hollander also appreciated the similarities between the East India Trading Company, as depicted in the story, and the modern world. "There's a contemporary parallel to how Lord Cutler Beckett and the East India Company operates in the story, with the pirates—who symbolize absolute freedom—being squeezed out ruthlessly. Especially Jack Sparrow," Hollander continues, "who in Beckett's view is naughty, messy, has dreadlocks, could do with a few more baths, and worst of all, is a pirate. To Cutler Beckett, Jack Sparrow is a stray dog."

The parallel of the East India Trading Company's efforts at world domination to the macroeconomic tendencies of today's culture actually helped him with his characterization. "I have a big map of the world that I'm obsessed with. As an actor, if you're playing a villain, you certainly want a big motivation. You don't just want to be casually violent," he says with a grin. "Though you're not quite sure whether he's simply working for the East India Trading Company or whether he's representing his own rule of law. His motives might be on a more personal level, and either way, he's after Jack's compass. It's something that will help him dominate the world, and he's not shy about making a deal with anyone to get it.

"He's very good at playing one character off against another," he continues. "He's very good at seeing what people's motivations are and what he can make them do. He sees something between Elizabeth and Jack he can exploit. He gets power over the governor by saying that's the only way that his daughter will be saved. He manipulates them all, and he can do all that from an armchair. He's very cold."

Is there anything nice about Lord Beckett? "Nothing," Hollander confirms. "He's just horrible. The only nice thing about him is that he's great fun to play. The devil always has the best tunes."

David Schofield
MERCER

David Schofield, the noted British character actor cast as Mercer, Lord Cutler Beckett's merciless enforcer, is a startling contrast to his on-screen character. The good-natured, good-humored, and greatly experienced Schofield recognized Mercer's soullessness, and then played it to the hilt. "On the surface, Lord Cutler Beckett is a rather charming character, like a lot of very powerful people. He's very well educated and seems like quite a nice chap. But there's a darker side, and I think Mercer is the instrument for his demons. Mercer is reserved, doesn't say much. Some people, I think, would find his quiet manner unsettling, and I should say that's with very good reason. Mercer is being asked by Beckett to solve problems with 'extreme prejudice.'

"Mercer is a force to be reckoned with," adds Schofield. "Beneath his ostensibly calm, collected, unruffled exterior, I think there's somebody who could truly be described as a psychopath." Ironically, Schofield was only too happy to play a man who speaks softly, if at all, and carries a very large stick, or at least, sword. "It's a great thrill to play a character like this. Less is more, for me, in the film world. I work a lot on the stage, and that's the place for talking, as far as I'm concerned. The movies are where you tell the story visually, and the less Mercer has to say, the better."

Naomie Harris
TIA DALMA
"Would you love me if I was anything but what I am?"

The mysterious Caribbean soothsayer Tia Dalma, a most compelling character, was introduced in *Dead Man's Chest*, to become an even more crucial element in *At World's End*. She's essayed by one of Britain's brightest and most beautiful young talents, Naomie Harris, who was excited by the possibilities of further flexing her burgeoning acting muscles.

"Tia Dalma's a free spirit, someone who has magic powers and the ability to see through people and understand their deepest desires," explains Naomie Harris. "She's a very powerful woman, which I really like. She has associations with the elements of nature, and she's fiery and temperamental. Tia Dalma doesn't do anything out of the goodness of her heart. She definitely wants something, which is only revealed in *At World's End*."

Harris had Tia Dalma pegged from the time she first auditioned for Gore Verbinski. "I only had two pages from the script before that audition," she recalls, "and just a little description of how Gore saw the character. I just kind of made up the character on my own, presented that to Gore, and thankfully, he loved it. And that was it. We never really deviated from that."

The character continued to take shape as the costume by Penny Rose, the hair by Martin Samuel, and the makeup by Ve Neill came into place. Harris was delighted with the results. "I didn't recognize myself at all when I looked in the mirror," she says gleefully. "And that's the way it should be. She has tribal markings, dreadlocks down to her waist, red eyes, and rotten teeth. Black ink oozes out of her mouth. It's so liberating not to care how you look. And the accent really helped to add to the character. My family is Jamaican, so I knew that accent well."

The young actress enjoyed the history and mystery of the calculating hoodoo practitioner. "[Jack and Tia] have a history together. He's an independent-spirited man, just like Tia Dalma. Which is what attracts them to each other in the beginning. We talked about this in the rehearsals, but it's not really in the script." As to that "touch of destiny," Will Turner? "She sees him as a key to her plan of salvation for herself, to regain her power.

"Also, I'm sure she could take on different forms. She's kind of a bit of everything, kind of really crazy and otherworldly. She's also good at just seeing into people's hearts and understanding what they truly want, as well. Yeah—she's a good person to go on a journey with."

THE CRITICAL CRITTERS

Well integrated with the human actors of the Pirates trilogy are the various beasts of the earth and air who make their own thespian impression on audiences. Few films in recent history have produced such sterling on-screen moments for non-humans, whether it be the Prison Dog reluctant to give up the key ring firmly embedded in its mouth to pleading prisoners, a screeching monkey named Jack who is fanatically devoted to his keeper or a classic pirate's parrot who does all of the talking for its mute owner. All of the creatures in the Pirates films were lovingly trained by animal coordinator Boone Narr, head trainer Mark Harden, and their team from Boone's Animals for Hollywood in Castaic, California. Working in Los Angeles was a virtual zoo, including in alphabetical order: crabs, dogs, donkeys, finches, fish, goats, iguanas, pigs—awake and sleeping, rats, seagulls, snakes, spiders, and a Vietnamese pot belly pig, who was undoubtedly vying for higher billing with the standard pigs. The menagerie that headed to the Caribbean for *Dead Man's Chest* and *At World's End* included two capuchin monkeys, two macaws, a dozen goats, three pigs, two white horses, two carriage horses, three dozen chickens, six cows, and fourteen ravens.

At His Bark and Call

The Prison Dog, a beloved character both in the original Pirates of the Caribbean attraction and then the films, was portrayed in *The Curse of the Black Pearl* by a delightful canine named Twister. By the time filming began on *Dead Man's Chest* and *At World's End* Twister had entered a well-

deserved retirement and was replaced by Chopper, a friendly and unbelievably smart eight-year-old terrier mix. However, Chopper needed time in the makeup trailer to correctly align the color of his coat with Twister's. "Chopper has an air-conditioned little trailer that he stays in, and sometimes he allows me to go inside," admits Boone Narr. "Then, on his day off, he expects me to run around and take care of him. I'm at his bark and call. He's got me well-trained."

Can We Squawk?

The silent Cotton's parrot was actually portrayed in *Dead Man's Chest* and *At World's End* by two macaws, spicy and spirited avian creatures appropriately named Chip and Salsa. "One's a good flyer, the other's a good sitter," notes David Bailie, who portrays the tongue-challenged pirate. "God, if you heard him squawk! You have no idea what that squawk is like at a two-inch range. Your head just rings."

TOP: Twister, the first Prison Dog, in *The Curse of the Black Pearl*; LEFT: The silent Cotton (David Bailie) and his ever-present, ever-talkative macaw.

important that he be the only one to have a close relationship with them. "Monkeys are incredibly social," he notes. "They have a very well established hierarchy, and what we try to do is keep them from thinking that the film set is a social situation, because they want to make contact with everybody there—find out who that person is and where they are in the hierarchy. So we teach the crew members to ignore the monkeys as much as possible, pretend they don't exist, even when the creatures start fluttering their eyes at them and try to open a social dialogue. And if that happens, the monkeys are going to make an opinion, and they can either love you or hate you and either one is bad for us.

"Because if they were to fall in love with Geoffrey Rush," Harden continues with a laugh, "we wouldn't get any work done. What the monkeys would express would be 'No, Geoffrey's my friend, I don't have to do any work.' And if they hated him, obviously that would spell disaster. So we don't give them the opportunity to make that opinion."

Of course, it's easier said than done, as nearly every single member of the cast and crew instantly fell head over heels for the adorable, chittering monkeys, recognizing them as not-so-distant relatives with their strangely human expressions and actions. *At World's End* really gave Pablo and Chiquita a chance to shine as simian thespians, such as being dressed in little Chinese costumes in the Singapore sequence, or stealing a Roman Candle and firing it during a pitched battle with East India Trading Company troops. "It was a literal blast," recalls Harden. "Pablo and Chiquita had to handle a lit candle and touch the flame to the wick, and it took over sixty takes to take it right. It wasn't just the monkeys, it was a harmonic convergence of all sorts of things going awry. But I was really happy. I mean, everybody teased me that it took sixty-six takes, but I was proud that the monkeys were willing to do it sixty-six times to get it right!"

Monkey Shines

As for everyone's favorite undead simian (who shares the same moniker as everyone's favorite pirate captain), "Jack" the Monkey—Captain Barbossa's best and perhaps only real friend—was portrayed by no fewer than four animal actors over the course of the three films. Tara (female) and Levi (male), both White-throated Capuchins, both played "Jack" in *The Curse of the Black Pearl*; Chiquita (female) and Pablo (male) took over those duties for both *Dead Man's Chest* and *At World's End*. Like Twister and Chopper, all four Capuchins needed not-so-extreme makeovers to suit the film's color palette. "We put a very safe vegetable dye to darken their white cowls," explains Mark Harden, "and ended up touching them up once a month."

Harden trained the monkeys through an astonishing series of actions throughout the films, and it was

TOP: Animal trainer Mark Harden of Boone's Animals for Hollywood; RIGHT: "Jack" the Monkey, even more of a mischief-maker than Captain Jack.

Creating the
Pirate World

Sets & Ships
AT LAND AND AT SEA

One of the things that makes moviemaking such a baffling yet wonderful process is that the artists who create the worlds that the characters and action inhabit are something like gods who can create these worlds from a void, sometimes in seven days, usually more, sometimes, under pressure, even less.

There were three basic foundations for the production design of the three films: the evocative look of the original Disney theme park attraction, the physical and architectural realities of the early eighteenth century and, of course, the imaginations of the director and the designers themselves.

THE CURSE OF THE BLACK PEARL

When I first got the call," says *The Curse of the Black Pearl* supervising art director Derek Hill, "I wondered—are we going real or are we going Disneyland?"

The answer was both. Gore Verbinski wanted to keep true to the essence of the attraction, while at the same time immersing the viewer in some of the realities of pirate life in the approximate period being depicted. "There were inspirations from old seafaring films that we'd seen," notes British-born production designer Brian Morris, "but we didn't harp on them too much. The [Disney] attraction really had a spirit about it, and it was great to have the underlying inspiration of the ride."

Morris and Hill collected a highly skilled team of artists and artisans, with construction coordinator Robert A. Blackburn coordinating a crew comprising some 280 carpenters, plasterers, painters, and laborers. When principal photography of *Pirates of the Caribbean: The Curse of the Black Pearl* commenced on October 9, 2002, the first sets were relatively modest compared to what would follow. The captain's cabin in the *Black Pearl* was constructed at KABC, a local news affiliate in Glendale, California. Several interiors in Governor Weatherby Swann's

OPPOSITE TOP: The crew of *The Curse of the Black Pearl* prepares to shoot aboard the first incarnation of the ship; OPPOSITE BOTTOM LEFT: Pirates swing on ropes from the *Black Pearl* to the Royal Navy's *Dauntless*; OPPOSITE BOTTOM RIGHT: Illustration of battling ships by Darek Gogol; ABOVE: The first *Black Pearl* evocatively lit by cinematographer Dariusz Wolski.

RIGHT: Giant, helium-elevated balloon lights were utilized to illuminate the *Black Pearl* at night; BELOW: Gore Verbinski addresses the crew and extras on the final set for *At World's End*, an intimidating fort constructed at the Golden Oak Ranch Disney in California; OPPOSITE: While *Black Pearl* pirates and Geoffrey Rush cavort on deck, crew members work belowdecks on the first version of the ship.

lavish Caribbean mansion were built at Raleigh Studios in Manhattan Beach (also in the Los Angeles area, despite its decidedly East Coast name). The location for the first major set piece to be constructed, Port Royal's Fort Charles, was on the Palos Verdes site of the shuttered Marineland of the Pacific, with an endless, 180-degree view of the Pacific Ocean. With no visible electrical wires, buildings, or roadways, the former tourist attraction proved an ideal spot to build the massive fort, including its stone walls, parapets, bell tower, officer's quarters, prison cell-block, and central courtyard (gallows included). "We prefabricated all of the parts and pieces of the fort in our North Hollywood mill and trucked them out to Palos Verdes, putting the fort together there," says Blackburn. "The fort had over 1,300 plaster 'skins' [squares or rectangles of prefabricated material that resembles brick or other building materials] which covered the set. The walls were framed up with plywood behind them, then the skins are put on. We knew that there was going to be a lot of talent up on the decks, so those were framed in lumber and heavy plywood, with a metal lathe and a concrete base over that. We used a stamping method, just like they stamp concrete for a driveway, because we had so much area to cover and so little time in which to do it."

When the company completed their work in Los Angeles and traveled to St. Vincent and the Grenadines for location shooting on January 9, 2003, Brian Morris and his team still had their work cut out for them—especially since the notion of

large-scale feature filmmaking on such remote and charmingly underdeveloped terrain meant that ninety-nine percent of the materials they needed had to be brought in by container ship. In beautiful Wallilabou Bay, Morris and Hill designed and constructed healthy chunks of Port Royal, including a wooden dock and Royal Navy building, and atmospheric pieces of Tortuga as well.

Pirate Treasure

The preeminent Los Angeles set for *The Curse of the Black Pearl*—based in part on the attraction's "Treasure Room"—was a massive cavern on the fictional *Isla de Muerta*, loaded with a cornucopia of booty looted by pirates from every corner of the globe. It's here where the two curse-lifting ceremonies take place, the last followed by a tremendous duel between Captains Jack Sparrow and Barbossa, ending with the latter's seeming demise. "Brian and Gore swung from one end of the spectrum to the other," says Jerry Bruckheimer. "A pirate lair is an utterly mythical place; creating a location like that is a dream come true for any creative mind. Of course, Brian and Gore had to consider specific action and story points, but as long as the cave was built as a workable space, they had carte blanche."

"We looked at caves from all over the world for reference," notes Morris. "There was a bit of this one, a bit of that one. We couldn't actually find a physical location we could work with, so we made a decision in the end to design and build it." Inhabiting nearly all of the 240-foot-long, 130-foot-wide environs of Stage 2 at the Walt Disney Studios, the treasure cave allowed Verbinski and Morris to create a quintessential pirate's hideaway. "In the twenty-eight years I've been doing this, the cave was kind of a new frontier," explains Bob Blackburn. For five

BELOW: Visual development of the Treasure Cave by Darek Gogol; OPPOSITE TOP: The massive treasure cave set was constructed on Stage 2 at the Walt Disney Studios; OPPOSITE BOTTOM: A reminder of "the opportune moment."

months, one hundred craftsman labored over the construction of the cave, and the tank in which it was built took on 300,000 gallons of water.

It was up to set decorator Larry Dias to adorn the cave (and the other sets) with all the necessary accoutrements of fantasy and reality. "The biggest challenge was definitely the treasure cave," Dias notes, "just trying to get the quantity of materials that Gore was looking for. It's a huge treasure. These pirates have been bringing stuff here for years, just literally dumping their treasure into the cave by the boatload. We were dealing with antiques and great objects, but handling them in a way that created disorder.

"Gore wanted gold everywhere," Dias continues. "He wanted it to be a magical reveal when the camera sees the interior of the cave for the first time. We manufactured almost one million coins, minted at places in Canada and in New Orleans by a person who makes doubloons for Mardi Gras. We minted actual *escudos*, the classic pieces of eight. I can't even think about how many cubic feet of rock we actually painted to look like gold nuggets. We also had hundreds of yards of pearls and beads." In all, it took three weeks with sixteen set dressers at any one time to fully dress the treasure-cave set.

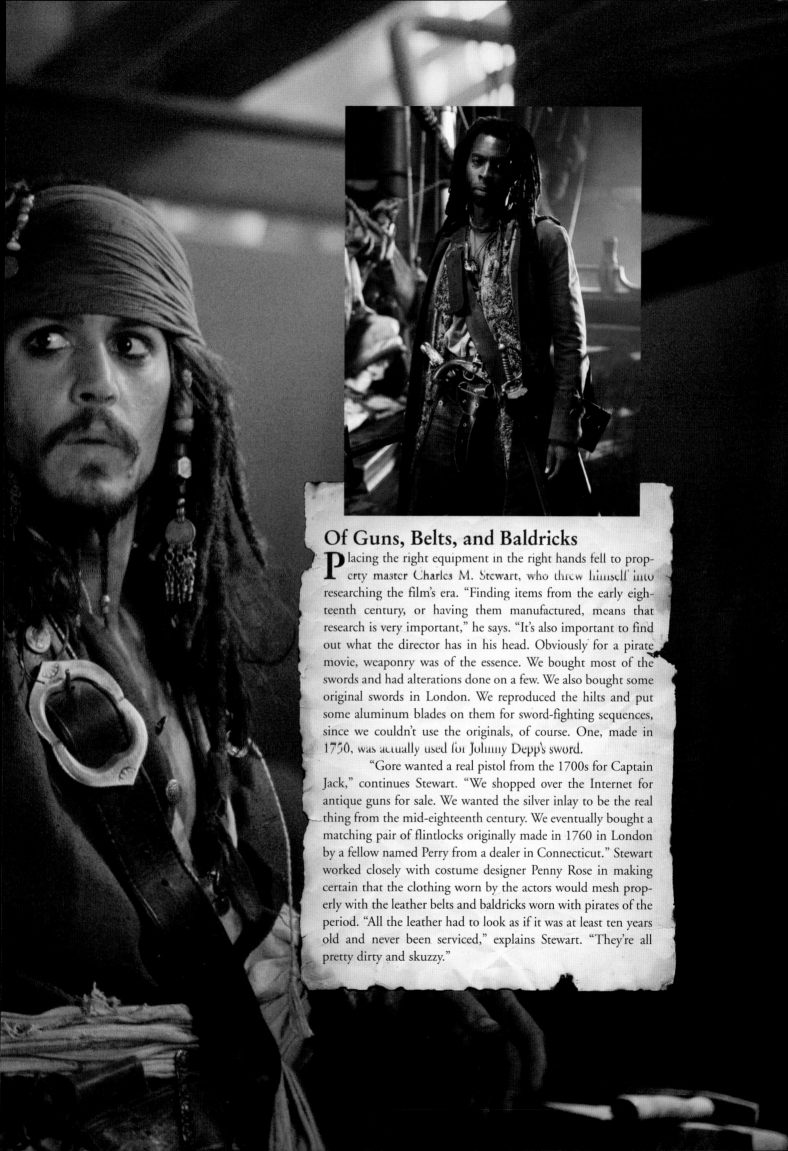

Of Guns, Belts, and Baldricks

Placing the right equipment in the right hands fell to property master Charles M. Stewart, who threw himself into researching the film's era. "Finding items from the early eighteenth century, or having them manufactured, means that research is very important," he says. "It's also important to find out what the director has in his head. Obviously for a pirate movie, weaponry was of the essence. We bought most of the swords and had alterations done on a few. We also bought some original swords in London. We reproduced the hilts and put some aluminum blades on them for sword-fighting sequences, since we couldn't use the originals, of course. One, made in 1750, was actually used for Johnny Depp's sword.

"Gore wanted a real pistol from the 1700s for Captain Jack," continues Stewart. "We shopped over the Internet for antique guns for sale. We wanted the silver inlay to be the real thing from the mid-eighteenth century. We eventually bought a matching pair of flintlocks originally made in 1760 in London by a fellow named Perry from a dealer in Connecticut." Stewart worked closely with costume designer Penny Rose in making certain that the clothing worn by the actors would mesh properly with the leather belts and baldricks worn with pirates of the period. "All the leather had to look as if it was at least ten years old and never been serviced," explains Stewart. "They're all pretty dirty and skuzzy."

~DAUNTLESS~ BLACK PEARL INTERCEPTOR

To the Victor Go the Spoils

At the same time the various sets were being built, three full-size ships were in various states of preparation for their starring and supporting roles in *The Curse of the Black Pearl*, primarily, of course, the titular one. Described by Brian Morris as "this mysterious, rotting, decaying beast," it is Captain Jack Sparrow's love of the *Black Pearl* and everything that it represents that sets the plot in motion. "The *Black Pearl* had to be the quintessential pirate ship," notes Jerry Bruckheimer. "Gore and I agreed it had to be iconic. Because this is the ship that's caused the lifelong feud between Jack and Barbossa, to the victor goes the spoils. The ship is a symbol of every treasure they've targeted." To the observant viewer, the *Black Pearl* also resembled, to some degree, a decrepit version of the theme park attraction's very own ship *Wicked Wench*, although a connection between the two was not to be explored until *At World's End* was made.

The *Black Pearl* was constructed twice for the first film. One version was mounted on a 105-foot by 28-foot barge that could be towed and another was built on a working gimbal for studio work inside of a humongous geodesic dome in Long Beach, California, that formerly housed Howard Hughes's Spruce Goose airplane.

Also constructed from the ground up for the first movie was the H.M.S. *Dauntless*, a powerful British warship commanded by Commodore James Norrington. "Our inspiration was the *Victory*, a wonderful-looking ship that represented the image of England in its time," notes Brian Morris. Sections of the *Dauntless* were built on a floating barge docked at Pier C in Long Beach over a three-and-a-half month period, before moving the launch to the Port of Los Angeles for filming. The *Dauntless* ultimately lived up to its name, measuring 170 feet long, 34 feet wide, and consisting of approximately 40,000 pounds of steel and 1,000 square feet of sails.

One ship that didn't have to be fabricated—only temporarily renovated—was the *Interceptor*, the two-masted clipper noted for its speed and stealth. Matt O'Connor, the marine coordinator for the first film, knew the perfect vessel to "play" the *Interceptor*—a magnificent old ship operated by the Gray's Harbor Historical Seaport Authority in the state of Washington, called, appropriately enough, *Lady Washington*. Of course, modifications were required to allow *Lady Washington* to make the often perilous 4,500-mile journey from Port Townsend, Washington, down to Long Beach, and then the challenging oceangoing trek to the island nation of St. Vincent and the Grenadines, the location in the far West Indies selected for *The Curse of the Black Pearl*. The ship was completely repainted, new hatch gratings were built, the number of gun ports was increased, and the steering apparatus was changed from a tiller to a wheel.

OPPOSITE: The *Black Pearl*, which has a lowered ramp to allow ship-to-ship transfers of people and equipment, readies for filming on the open sea; ABOVE: Conceptual illustrations by Jim Byrkit of the three principal ships of the first film.

DEAD MAN'S CHEST

The simultaneous shooting of *Pirates of the Caribbean: Dead Man's Chest* and *At World's End* began on February 28, 2005, with studio and location work in Los Angeles. As with *The Curse of the Black Pearl*, the first few sets were relatively modest: a piece of the Turkish prison that opens the film (to be considerably expanded later by the wizards at ILM), the rum locker of the *Black Pearl*, and the interior of the Port Royal jailhouse. New production designer Rick Heinrichs's large-scale masterworks followed soon afterwards.

"I got excited when I first met with Gore," recalls Heinrichs, "because I found him sketching pirate ships in a sketchbook. He's a very visual director who is himself able to draw, and that's very rare. Gore said that he wanted to take what had been established in the first film to a whole other level of mythology." While respecting and often building upon Brian Morris's designs from the first *Pirates* film, Heinrichs and his team sought to "take things as far as we could to make the settings real living things," according to supervising art director John Dexter. "That's why so much of the research we did was from natural forms."

Heinrichs, along with Dexter, three art directors, seven assistant art directors, nine set designers, one props set designer, three conceptual artists, six illustrators, three model makers, and various and sundry graphic designers, coordinators, researchers, and assistants—not to mention affiliated departments headed by set decorator Cheryl Carasik, property master Kristopher E. Peck, and construction coordinator Greg Callas—would achieve wonders on land and sea for *Dead Man's Chest* and *At World's End*. A visit to the Pirates art department at the Walt Disney Studios in Burbank during pre-production revealed detailed models, mountains of reference books, conceptual illustrations, blueprints, and walls plastered from one end to the other with reference artwork—from old paintings and etchings of ships, seas, and landscapes to ethnographic photographs, design sketches, and highly inspirational reproductions of Howard Pyle illustrations from his classic *Book of Pirates*.

A Good Place for a Fight

Once again back on the versatile grounds of the former Marineland in Palos Verdes, in pretty much the exact spot where the Port Royal fort had stood for *The Curse of the Black Pearl*, Heinrichs designed and built a Port Royal church for the opening scene of *Dead Man's Chest*, in which Will and Elizabeth's wedding is rudely interrupted.

Leaping a few miles to the Universal Studios backlot, Rick Heinrichs, John Dexter, Cheryl Carasik, and their teams accomplished another extreme makeover of its "Europe street" area, converting it into the atmospheric Tortuga cantina in which Captain Jack and Joshamee Gibbs search for souls to populate the *Flying Dutchman* in *Dead Man's Chest*, climaxing in a good, old-fashioned barroom brawl.

OPPOSITE: Atmospheric visual development by Aaron McBride and Rick Heinrichs of the Turkish prison that opens *Dead Man's Chest*; ABOVE: Howard Pyle illustration from his 1903 *Book of Pirates*.

Beckett's Headquarters

The primary set in the new and improved Port Royal was Lord Cutler Beckett's imposing headquarters, with a huge map of the world clearly dictating his "today the Caribbean, tomorrow the world" philosophy. "We were re-visiting the Port Royal set from *The Curse of the Black Pearl*," notes Rick Heinrichs, "and the challenge was to let the audience know they were in the same place, but that some period of time had passed. The original set was still there at Wallilabou Bay in St. Vincents two years after they shot the first film, and we were going to use what was left. Ironically, not two months before we shot there on the second and third films, a tremendous surge came up and knocked the remaining sets into the water. So we *had* to do a complete reconstruction."

Voodoo Shacks

The company spent a week at the studio shooting the huge Pantano River set with Tia Dalma's tumbledown but richly decorated tree house as its centerpiece. This set was a truly magical evocation of a Caribbean swampland river, lined with stark, overhanging trees and brush, and rickety lean-tos—a deliberate tip of the hat to the bayou in the original Disneyland Pirates of the Caribbean attraction. "I remember as a kid watching the episode of *The Wonderful World of Color* that introduced the Pirates ride," recalls Rick Heinrichs, "and being totally blown away by it at the time. The opportunity to be involved with something that references this is, in my mind, a tribute to the designers such as Marc Davis and others who did such incredible work. It was such a pleasure to be able to do that." In truth, working on Pirates was something of a homecoming to Heinrichs, whose first job in Hollywood was as an Imagineer at Disney's WED Enterprises when many of the original Pirates of the Caribbean attraction creators were still working there.

"The Pantano River set at Disney was designed to match the actual location chosen in Dominica for the Indian River sequence," explains construction coordinator Greg Callas. "The bloodwood trees that border this river are extraordinary, and we replicated them on stage from steel, car foam, and plaster with silk leaves on it, which required a lot of work. We also built an aboveground tank above the stage floor that we filled with half a million gallons of water. It actually created the right sense of humidity for the 'location.'"

Tia Dalma's shack is lined from end-to-end and top-to-bottom with the bric-a-brac of her artful profession. "I've never done a hoodoo, voodoo, scary 1720-ish bayou interior before," says set decorator Cheryl Carasik with a laugh.

BELOW: First assistant director Peter Kohn places background players in the massive Pantano River set built on Stage 2; OVERLEAF: Tia Dalma accepts Captain Jack's gift of the undead "Jack" the Monkey.

105

"Gore wanted a lot of texture hung from the ceiling so we prepped bottles encrusted with jewels, along with dried herbs. Inside the bottles were spiders, eyeballs, and mushrooms that actually started growing over a period of time. There was also a lot of taxidermy all over the place."

It was no coincidence, then, that this set drew a visit from the legendary Francis Xavier "X" Atencio, the Disney Legend who, along with other Imagineers, wrote the script for the original theme park attraction, as well as the lyrics to George Bruns's music for what is now the world's most famous sea shanty, "Yo Ho (A Pirate's Life for Me)." The Pirates film company rolled out the red carpet for "X," honoring him with his own director's chair, with Jerry Bruckheimer, Gore Verbinski, Johnny Depp, Orlando Bloom, Keira Knightley, and a long parade of cast and crew paying due homage. "Without this man," spoke Verbinski for one and all, "none of us would be here right now."

A New and Improved *Black Pearl*

Constructed in Bayou La Batre, Alabama—famed for its shipyards and expert shipbuilders—was the brand-new, fully seaworthy, and subtly re-designed *Black Pearl*. "We took the *Black Pearl* and gave it a little bit more of a swoop," says Heinrichs. "The *Black Pearl* in the first film was established, to some degree, by the set of circumstances that they had. They built the ship directly onto a barge and were limited by the dimensions of that barge. Gore wanted a much more flexible *Pearl* that could move faster than one or two knots."

The new *Black Pearl* was built around an existing 109-foot-long boat called the *Sunset*, an unglamorous craft that once serviced oil derricks in the Gulf of Mexico. After eight months of construction, something familiar yet brand new had been created. "In this movie, the *Pearl* is a much sexier, cooler, edgier ship than last time," adds supervising art director John Dexter.

The gun and hold decks of the *Black Pearl* were constructed with extraordinary realism inside of Walt Disney Studios Soundstage 1, the burnished wood looking like it had been weathered on rough seas for fifty years rather than a few weeks. When outfitted by set decorator Cheryl Carasik with the appropriate accoutrements, such as crisscrossing hammocks on the hold deck, and period-correct baskets, ropes, and gently swinging lanterns, the illusion of reality was complete. Four hydraulic pistons mounted on a gimbal on opposite sides of the set provided a rolling motion effectively mimicking the sea, providing the cast and crew with a milder preview of what would come later while shooting in the Caribbean.

The captain's cabin on both the *Black Pearl* and *Edinburgh Trader* were constructed at the studio for interior sequences. The former set was based upon Brian Morris's original designs but rebuilt in solid mahogany, which lent it an even more lustrous look and feel.

ABOVE: Disney Legend X. Atencio visits Johnny Depp on the Pantano River bayou set; OPPOSITE ABOVE: The re-built *Black Pearl* at full sail in the Caribbean. The upper part of the sails were added later by ILM via computer graphics; RIGHT: Pintel and Ragetti blast away at the Kraken; FAR RIGHT: Gore Verbinski, on the gun deck, gives directions to actors on the brig deck below on the new, two-deck, gimbaled interior of the *Pearl*.

Flying Dutchman

Also under construction at this point for filming later in both Dominica and the Bahamas was the stupendous *Flying Dutchman*, 170 feet and 420 tons of brute nautical force. "When we design and build a set," says Rick Heinrichs, "we try to get a real sense of place and history to it by using colors and textures that hopefully add character and have something behind the actors that will make them feel as if they're really in the environment. I think we reached that zenith with the *Flying Dutchman*. We wanted it to be an actual character in the film. We put a lot of sea forms everywhere—ferns, mollusks, barnacles, and all the stuff that grows underwater. Whenever it was being shot, they wet down the boat to make sure it felt alive."

Her sails were shredded into shards; a skeletal, almost crocodilian figure resembling a terrifying predator was installed on the bow; and her rotting wooden decks were decorated with the detritus of the Seven Seas. Thirty-six sea life–encrusted but fully operational cannons were constructed on either side of her hull as well as two revolving triple gun cannons that would emerge from her bow to threaten any and all who dared to stray into her path.

The *Flying Dutchman* was partially inspired by old Dutch *fluyts*—seventeenth-century vessels that resembled galleons, and specifically, the *Vasa*, a massive Swedish warship that sunk in Stockholm's harbor upon its maiden voyage in 1628. (The ship was salvaged in 1961 and is now housed in a special museum in the Swedish capital.) With its high, heavily ornamented stern, the *Vasa* provided a rich foundation for Rick Heinrichs's wilder and more fantastical designs.

Working closely with Heinrichs, as he has for years, was construction coordinator Greg Callas, at the head of a department which, at its height, included some 450 craftsmen, encompassing carpenters, plasterers, painters, landscapers, and sculptors. "I'd never built a ship before, and there's a whole glossary of terms you have to learn to understand a wooden pirate ship," explains Callas. "We had to manufacture the capstan and the wheel, fife rail, mizzenmast, mainmast, and foremast. Things I'd never imagined. Our marine department helped make the

ABOVE: The "capstan hammer," which summons the Kraken; RIGHT: The *Flying Dutchman*, sails unfurled, rendered by production designer Rick Heinrichs.

PAGES 112–113: The *At World's End* company prepares to film from a specially built shooting platform below the stern of the *Flying Dutchman*; INSET: The *Flying Dutchman*, moored at the "210 dock," so-called because of its 210-foot-long length, on Grand Bahama Island.

On the *Dutchman* Sets

*Overgrown with barnacles and mussels, her halls
decked with boughs of seaweed, the* Flying Dutchman
*plies its deathly trade across the Seven Seas. "The ship
alone is worth your entrance fee to the movie," says
Bill Nighy. "It's hard to distinguish between the crew
members and the boat, and the crew serves in a way
that seamen generally don't serve. You are required to
do things that humans should not be required to do.
You are in a half-life, a limbo between life and death.
The* Dutchman *spends a degree of time under the sea,
as well as on top of it, so we exist in a rare state.
When I first saw it, I found it humbling. It's without
doubt one of the most creative sets for a movie I've
ever come across in my life."*

vessels run with diesel motors, and a rigging department outfitted everything with sails. Rigging today is done with cables, but on these ships, it's all period rigging with ropes. The sails had to be created according to eighteenth-century-period specifications, then everything had to be aged to look old. You don't just go down to a marine store and buy this stuff! Everything we did had to be manufactured." The *Black Pearl* and the *Flying Dutchman* were each constructed up to their first set of fighting tops, with four complete sets of sails. The remainder of the masts and sails would be supplied later by Industrial Light & Magic.

The sequences inside of Davy Jones's cabin on the *Flying Dutchman* can best be described as "Underwater Gothic." "The cabin certainly has a very operatic feel to it," says Heinrichs. "Jones plays an enormous pipe organ we designed and built from scratch. It plays as a normal organ would, but the pipes have grown fantastically into all of these underwater shapes, with steam coming out of them. The organ itself has shell and sea life textures, backed up to the window of the stern. We also designed a painting above the organ keys that has a weirdly sweet and romantic feel to it. That was intentional, because we were trying to give Davy Jones's character some pathos, because he's mourning a lost love."

Back to the Bay

When the *Dead Man's Chest/At World's End* company traveled to the Caribbean at the end of February 2005, once again beautiful Wallilabou Bay in St. Vincent and the Grenadines would be the locale for both the Port Royal and Tortuga exteriors. Heinrichs and his team re-created Port Royal in even greater detail than in the first film, with the added structures of the East India Trading Company dock and offices. Anchored in the bay was an impressive array of period vessels, dominated by the 169-foot, full-rig H.M.S. *Bounty*, which in *Dead Man's Chest* "portrays" the *Edinburgh Trader*, an ill-fated merchant ship destined for a most unpleasant encounter with the Kraken. The *Bounty*, like its real-life namesake, has an extraordinary history of its own. She was built for Metro-Goldwyn-Mayer's epic 1962 version of *Mutiny on the Bounty* starring Marlon Brando, Trevor Howard, and Richard Harris. For that film, the ship made the 7,327-mile voyage from Lunenburg to Tahiti in thirty-three sailing days, via the Panama Canal. Forty-three years later, the *Bounty*, under Captain Robin R. Walbridge, would sail a mere 2,096 statute miles (1,821 nautical miles) in fourteen days from Bayou La Batre—where she was being re-fitted and re-painted as the *Edinburgh Trader*—to St. Vincent, with stops along the way in Miami, Florida, and Mayaguez, Puerto Rico, for fuel and provisions.

Supervised by coordinator Will White, the *Bounty* was joined in Wallilabou Bay by several more "picture boats" from near and far, among them *Providence* (a 110-foot topsail fighting sloop); *St. Peter* (a 74-foot schooner from Antigua); and *Unicorn* (a 145-foot bark from St. Lucia that portrayed the *Terpsichore*). The support flotilla in "Walli" included twelve boats of various kinds, not to mention some dozen British longboats faithfully reconstructed from original eighteenth-century plans.

ABOVE: Davy Jones's cabin, built on Stage 2 at the Walt Disney Studios; RIGHT: Neil Panlasigui as a hungry Pelegostos boy waiting for Captain Jack to be served up.

The Village of the Pelegostos

Filming in Dominica began in mid-April 2005, on the island's Hampstead Beach, a bucolic stretch of sand overlooking a glistening turquoise sea on the northeast coast, backed by a lush, tangled jungle and coconut palm groves. In fact, some of it had been created just for the film, with art director William Ladd Skinner bringing in some 7,000 plants, primarily non-edible dasheen and transplanted palms.

South of the Dominican capital of Roseau is an aerie appropriately called High Meadow. It, along with a nearby spot called Twin Peaks, which overhangs the main road, was selected as the location for the richly and wittily designed native village of the Pelegostos, a wholly tongue-in-cheek, fictitious creation (as is the island they live on) inspired by pirate folklore.

"One of the great things that the writers and Gore have done with the concept of the Pelegostos village," says Heinrichs, "is to create this wonderful escape episode that puts the pirates into a completely absurd but funny set of circumstances that becomes a comedy of errors. Part of the physical comedy is that the village is set way up in the mountains, with the huts on top of different pitons with rope bridges between one and the other. The huts themselves are an organic riff on a skull, with eye and mouth holes, and everything brought up into a bun at the top. It gives a kind of animus to the entire village."

The Pelegostos village is a highly inventive pastiche of primitive designs laced with a mordant sense of humor. In addition to the twined branches, which compose the native huts, much of the village is constructed and decorated with the materials left over from the Pelegostos's enemies—that is, bones and other residue.

ABOVE RIGHT: Production designer Rick Heinrichs in front of one of his witty Pelegostos habitations; ABOVE LEFT: Natsuko Ohama (sitting, left) and other background players, arrayed as Pelegostos, wait for the next set-up in Dominica.

Instead of beaded curtains in the entrance of the circular doorways to give their inhabitants some privacy, they're fabricated with small bones instead. "What goes through my mind when I remember the Pelegostos village is 385 skulls," laughs Cheryl Carasik. Skulls are a major motif, used in all sorts of ways that Martha Stewart never even imagined (but might very well admire). "The local people we hired were fantastic," Carasik continues. "We had two guys who didn't miss a beat. We'd say that we needed some vines to wrap on the joints of Pelegostos furniture that we'd made, and off they'd go into the bush and come back two hours later with an armful of them." The long and very rickety-looking rope bridge linking one side of the village to the other looks treacherous—and, in fact, *felt* treacherous when walking over it and viewing the sheer sixty-foot drop below—but it was a marvelous illusion. Strong steel pilings supported the bridge, making it as safe as crossing the Golden Gate. Construction coordinator Greg Callas actually imported a construction team from Las Vegas that has built suspension bridges at theme parks and zoos throughout the world.

"For the Pelegostos huts, we had to build a shell, a superstructure, of very

ABOVE: Gore Verbinski discusses the shot of Will Turner being carried into the Pelegostos village with cinematographer Dariusz (Darek) Wolski; BELOW: Development illustration by James Carson of the Pelegostos village; OPPOSITE: Illustration by Jim Carson of pirates imprisoned in the dangling Bone Cage.

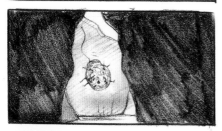

lightweight material to get its initial shape," explains Callas. "Then we manufactured some fiberglass skins that looked like roots and tree limbs to put over the top. Then we wrapped the whole thing with real roots and tree limbs, so these huts became incredibly heavy when we had to move them." To get the trucks up to the Pelegostos village location, Callas had to build a fifteen-degree road up the hillside. "There's no road in Dominica that's fifteen degrees," he notes. "That's almost straight up! It's pretty radical, but we got all our trucks and crew up there."

Atop a ridge in a spot called Vielle Casse, with a magnificent unspoiled view of the ocean, Rick Heinrichs designed a ruined, abandoned church and adjacent broken-down mill wheel and graveyard that became the setting for the spectacular stunt-action sequence on *Isla Cruces* in *Dead Man's Chest*. "The location is like a peninsula, surrounded on three sides by the ocean," explains Greg Callas. "I asked, 'where's the equipment going to go?' They said, 'don't worry about that, just build the set.'" It took Callas and company four months to construct the dilapidated church, which stands at the height of a six-story building.

To access the Vielle Casse location, one actually had to walk down a thirty degree graded road from the main thoroughfare, which was not accessible by most vehicles. The downhill walk in the intense heat wasn't so bad—but going up again after a twelve hour day of sizzling in the tropical sun was something else. "This is all part of the Pirates fitness program," joked unit production manager Doug Merrifield. "You don't need a gym membership. You just need to work on Pirates of the Caribbean. Gore and Jerry will get you into great shape!"

LEFT: Jim Byrkit storyboards of the Bone Cage rolling into the gorge; BELOW: Crew members carry the Bone Cage to a site in the Dominican jungle.

Mastering the Props

Typical of the film's attention to minute detail was the enormous amount of goods that spilled out from property master Kris Peck's truck. At one point, Peck had eight prop trucks spread across four countries in which *Dead Man's Chest* and *At World's End* were filming, waiting to supply whatever was necessary to appropriately outfit an actor, extra, or stunt player. Much of Peck's work was done in collaboration with Rick Heinrichs's art department, or, if there were mechanics involved, with special effects and other technical divisions. For the pistols, swords, daggers, and other weaponry, Peck worked closely with armorers Kelly Farrah and Harry Lu, and Peter Twist, who served as historical adviser on the three Pirates films. Although many of the weapons are replicas or are realistically fabricated from latex and other materials, Captain Jack Sparrow's sword was the same 1750 model that *The Curse of the Black Pearl* propmaster Charles Stewart had found for him on the first film. "We had 300 swords, and they were all manufactured for these movies," notes Peck. "The pirates' swords were dirty and grungy. Then we had dress swords for characters such as Commodore James Norrington and Governor Weatherby Swann. Our *Flying Dutchman* crewmen had swords encrusted with oceanic life."

LEFT: An array of well-encrusted weaponry used by Davy Jones's crewmen; BELOW: Ragetti peers into a jar of eyeballs in Tia Dalma's shack.

The Dead Man's Chest

Perhaps the most important prop of all was the titular object—the Dead Man's Chest itself—designed with intricate nautical motifs. "Gore made it very clear to us that since this was the title that was going to be on every billboard, poster, bus-stop bench, and grocery-store line, he wanted us to get it as right as possible," says Kris Peck. "This integrated more departments than any prop I've ever worked on—the writers, the illustrators, the production designer, the sculptors, and the molders. Then it went on to the prop shop for the mechanics. It had to look unbreakable, like a cast-iron skillet."

119

AT WORLD'S END

Although several location scenes for *At World's End* had already been shot in St. Vincent, Dominica, The Exumas, and Grand Bahama Island, early September 2005 saw the filming of its first major stage set piece. For many, the set represented the apotheosis of the artistry of Rick Heinrichs and his entire department: a massive, fanciful interpretation of Singapore in the early eighteenth century.

Constructed at Universal Studios, this amazing funhouse of a set, consisting of some forty individual structures, was built on top of an 80-foot by 130-foot tank. It was comprised of a harbor replete with Southeast Asian thatched huts, houses built on stilts (known as kampongs), and a swath of the fabled city itself, more formally Chinese in design, including a marketplace, an adjacent street where all sorts of dubious business takes place, and a vast bathhouse frequented by local pirates. Heinrichs also designed and built the low-roofed area underneath the bathhouse where workers keep the water heated with large furnaces. This was the stage for an early and crucial sequence in *At World's End* in which Will, Elizabeth, and Barbossa try to attain the map that could lead them to Davy Jones's Locker—and therefore to Captain Jack Sparrow, who was sent there by the Kraken at the finale of *Dead Man's Chest*. What ensues is a tremendous action sequences that spills from the town area onto the rickety boardwalks that connect the kampong houses, pitting the pirates against soldiers of the East India Trading Company.

"[Our] Singapore is a mélange of different influences and architectural styles that we researched when we were studying what Singapore might have looked like at that time," says Heinrichs. "Singapore was not a particularly well-documented place until the nineteenth century, so we looked at a number of other Chinese cities for reference during our time frame. We took a deliberately fantastical approach, creating something of a Chinese/Malaysian expressionist style.

"The bathhouse is a nasty example of hygiene that pokes fun at the spa sensibility running rampant today," continues Heinrichs. "We have a lot of mushrooms and other fungi growing out of the wooden tubs, and in fact, the pirates have spent so much time lazing around the tubs that they also have mushrooms growing out of *them*! They don't seem to leave their filthy ways on the ships; they bring them with them into the bathhouse. This gives you a wonderful sense of what

OPPOSITE TOP: Picture boat coordinator Will White pushes a camera craft through the massive Singapore set while East India Trading Company soldiers cross a bridge above them; OPPOSITE BOTTOM: Conceptual illustration of the kampong stilt houses in the Singapore set by James Carson; BOTTOM: Mushrooms grow not only on the wooden tubs of the world's grottiest bathhouse, but also on the pirates who inhabit them.

PREVIOUS PAGES: The
Empress, Captain Sao
Feng's flagship, con-
structed atop a steel
barge, in front of the cameras off the coast of
Grand Bahama Island;
ABOVE: The market and
town section of the Singapore set, built inside Universal Studios' Stage 12;
RIGHT: Elizabeth Swann
exquisitely dressed in elegant Chinese finery for
her rendezvous with Cap-
tain Sao Feng.

filthy beasts and brutes the pirates are. We've added lots of thickeners and color to the water so that it looks unwholesome. We also gave the floor of the bathhouse a meandering, planked look that's seemingly organic. To do that, every floorboard had to be hand cut."

Cheryl Carasik's set decoration, half of which was actually imported from Asia, was an incredible grab bag of painted scrolls, hanging laundry, food products, and flicker-ing Chinese lanterns, as well as crates, barrels, buckets, bas-kets, and bushels, all made of rattan, bamboo (much of which Carasik brought back from the Dominican locations), wood, and palm fronds, just as they would be in Southeast Asia. Atmospherically, the Singapore set actually *felt* like Southeast Asia, with heavy, dripping humidity caused by the thousands of gallons of water in the tank utilized to create the harbor area combined with the heat emanating from the powerful lighting equipment. There was even a visible fog that could always be seen just above the water level.

More Ships (Junks Included)

Much of *At World's End* is set on the sea, and in addition to the *Black Pearl* and the *Flying Dutchman*, Heinrichs had additional ships to design for the film. While the *Empress* and the *Hai Peng* are both Chinese junks, they are a study in contrasts. The *Empress* is the elaborately decorated flagship of Singaporean pirate Captain Sao Feng (Chow Yun-Fat); the *Hai Peng* is a much more modest affair, a junk that really *looks* like junk, composed of rotting, decrepit wood and thatched roofing on its deck structure. "For the *Empress*, we used the idea of Captain Sao Feng as something of a peacock," notes Heinrichs, "so there are design elements that reflect that, such as the long arc of its shape, which seems to almost swoop up into a tail on the rear of the ship. There are sail extensions on the sides of the ship that are almost like feathers that could help to drive the ship forward." Sao Feng's elaborate cabin on the *Empress* was constructed on a soundstage and layered with sensual fabrics, a multitude of burning candles for atmospheric lighting, and a moon-gate entrance.

Fully half of the *Endeavour*, Lord Cutler Beckett's imposing East India Trading Company flagship, was constructed and filmed on Grand Bahama Island, with the remainder added by CG imagery. Beckett's cabin on the ship was constructed in the Studio, its design reflecting his vaulted view of himself as someone

ABOVE: Visual development art of the *Empress* by Nathan Schroeder.

Keep To The *Pirata Codex*

"**K**eep to the Code" is an oft-heard slogan in the Pirates films, but in *At World's End*, the audience actually gets a chance to see the real deal. "The Pirate Code book had to be grand and spectacular," explains property master Kris Peck. "I wanted to put a lot of detail in it. Tom Mallory, who writes for a San Diego newspaper, wrote the text based upon the work from Ted Elliott and Terry Rossio, things I'd discovered in my research, or story points that needed to be factored in." Peck and Mark Van Stone, an expert in ancient calligraphy and manuscripts, combed through the archives of UCLA for inspiration. "We studied them microscopically. Parchment was scarce back then, so they would scratch off the ink and write over it, or sew additions on top of the original paper. We put ourselves in the pirate world—wondering what they would be doing as it was recorded. Maybe a parrot on someone's shoulder dropped sunflower seeds into the middle of the book. Or ashes from a pipe became ingrained into the paper." After Peck, Mallory, and Van Stone completed their "first draft," James Ward Byrkit illustrated it and added other materials. "Jim laid wonderful stuff into the character and texture of the Pirate Code," says Peck, "We have recipes for beer, how to attack a ship, or where you can find the best brothel in Singapore. We have wine stains, blood stains, wax stamps and seals, and addendums actually sewn onto the parchment pages." The final dimensions of the *Pirata Codex* were twenty by twenty-eight inches, with the embossed cover an inch bigger, weighing some eighty pounds. "So we made a second book," Peck continues, "because we had these two little, old, long-bearded men who have to carry it. The Keeper of the Code needed something easier to work with as well. So the second version weighed only about ten pounds."

making over the entire world. "There's sort of a Chaplinesque *Great Dictator* aspect to Beckett," says Heinrichs, "which we can see in the huge globe that's in his cabin, kind of a counterpart to the big map of the world that's in his Port Royal office. On Beckett's desk in the cabin are toy ships and navigational devices that intentionally resemble instruments of torture. He not only has the world in a vise, but he's going to flay it as well."

The last of the fabulous sets built was Shipwreck Cove, where the raucous and divisive Brethren Court of Pirate Lords meets to make a last plan of action against the onslaughts of Beckett and the East India Trading Company armada.

"Shipwreck Cove was conceived by Gore as a kind of retirement home for old pirates, comprised of the wrecked hulls of various ships hidden in a volcano," notes Heinrichs. "The Brethren Court meets in one of those hulls, and outside of the structure we've extended the set with a 300-foot long backing that is beautifully designed and painted in the good, old-fashioned Hollywood tradition."

The Brethren Court

Shipwreck City now took over Stage 2 of the Walt Disney Studios, where the great treasure cave and Pantano River sets had previously resided.

On Heinrichs's evocative set, rickety boardwalks connect one rotting old hull to another, with the Court's meeting place gorgeously illuminated by 800 three-wick candles. Decorative figureheads from plundered ships have been used for target practice, pierced by an amusing array of swords, hatchets, and daggers by the rowdy Pirate Lords. The filming of the sequence was pretty raucous itself. The set was crammed with nearly all of the film's stars, a wildly colorful array of Pirate Lords, their retainers, and henchmen from the Seven Seas. The members of the Court hailed from the likes of Spain, France, North and Equatorial Africa, China, and India and were portrayed by some very distinguished international actors, including Syria's Ghassan Massoud, who coincidentally portrayed Saladin opposite Orlando Bloom in *Kingdom of Heaven.*

A key member of the Court was Captain Teague, Keeper of the Code in the *Pirata Codex,* as set forth by the legendary Morgan and Bartholomew themselves, to which even the most dastardly buccaneer must religiously adhere. Teague is also a man who may share some DNA with Captain Jack, as evidenced by a certain similarity of behavior, wardrobe, and attitude.

So the casting was pre-ordained. For nearly a year, rumors flew that it would be none other than Keith Richards, legendary guitarist of the Rolling Stones, and a close mate of Johnny Depp . . . who had admittedly modeled much of Captain Jack Sparrow on his great and good friend. And the rumors, for a refreshing change, were true.

"The sort of connection I made when first thinking about Captain Jack," notes Depp, "was the idea that pirates were the rock and roll stars of that era. Their myths or legends would arrive months before they would ever make port, much like rock stars."

OPPOSITE: As Captain Jack watches, Keeper of the Code Captain Teague, portrayed by Keith Richards, takes the key for the *Pirata Codex* offered by the Prison Dog during the meeting of the Brethren Court; ABOVE RIGHT: From the pages of the *Pirata Codex.*

127

ABOVE: Keith Richards strums the guitar created by Danny Farrington at the behest of propmaster Kris Peck. BELOW: Keith Richards and Gore Verbinski chat on the Shipwreck City set.

Richards was understandably somewhat wary at first of accepting the role of Captain Teague. "When I first heard about it, I was thinking, oh, my God, this is an Elvis Presley thing. You pop in and sing. But when I saw how it fit into the whole scenario, then it felt quite natural to do it. It's about freedom, baby," adds Richards. "Open the cage, let the tigers out. Somebody's gotta do the naughty work. It's not so much about destroying the establishment. It's to prevent them from destroying *you*. And," he notes, "they've also made me a lovely guitar."

Strumming that guitar—especially designed and built for him by the legendary instrument maker Danny Farrington at the request of propmaster Kris Peck—and wielding a mean flintlock pistol, Richards took the company by hurricane force. "It was kind of a longshot to even think about getting Keith to do this," says Depp. "The fact that he agreed was above and beyond a dream come true. Experiencing his arrival on set was unbelievable. Every single person on the crew, including people you hadn't seen in months, suddenly showed up. It was a beautiful, perfect symmetry."

As for the unique connection between Captains Sparrow and Teague, Depp notes, "You get the feeling that there was a real tough-love relationship there. Teague is one of those pirates who would give you a hug one minute and blow you away the next. Or maybe he'll blow you away and *then* give you a hug. You don't know what to expect from him."

Jim Byrkit and His Magical Map

One of Gore Verbinski's closest collaborators is James Ward Byrkit, who has made indelible contributions to the director's films, first as a storyboard artist and then as much more. "For Pirates, we discussed the script, story, themes, character beats, things that went beyond traditional storyboarding." Byrkit's title on Pirates is "conceptual consultant" because, "What I was doing became a lot more than just storyboards."

Byrkit drew the first artwork of the *Black Pearl*. In addition to storyboards for the second two Pirates films, he also worked with the production design, props, and pre-visualization departments, helping with simplified animatics of the action sequences, which were a blueprint for Verbinski on the set, and later, for ILM's visual effects.

"In July 2005, Gore called a big meeting with everybody," recalls Byrkit. "He knew that he needed this great map [for *At World's End*]. He knew that it had to be something we hadn't seen before, with its own secrets. One idea was that if you shone a light underneath it, it would project this whole universe on the ceiling. Another was a pop-up book in which you pulled the center of the map out like a Chinese lantern. I actually bought some lanterns and tried to paint a globe on them, but it didn't work.

"An earlier idea we had was a circular map with rings that represented the metaphorical places to which you could travel. There are places in the world that are *Terra Incognita*—lands that are unknown—so they could have monsters, they could have magic, they could have new civilizations.

"When I showed the mock-up of it to Gore," Byrkit continues, "he said 'That's it! Now, not only do the rings move, but you need land masses that become shapes.' It took almost eight months to make the elements work right. The rings can line up in infinite ways, like a combination lock, and each way reveals some new secret, some unexplored place, some parallel universe.

RIGHT: The Map to the Land of the Dead, created by James Ward Byrkit, then refined by a coterie of *At World's End* production personnel, from propmaster Kris Peck to genius standby painter Tony Leonardi.

Kris Peck created mechanics that make the rings turn in an entirely "practical" manner, with no CGI enhancements. "The inner workings of the map underneath are really beautiful," enthuses Byrkit, "like a grandfather clock.

"Several hundred phrases needed to be translated into Chinese calligraphy, so propmaster Kris Peck brought in expert J.C. Brown. The original painting was done on *washi*—handmade Japanese rice paper—treated with layer upon layer of transparent washes of watercolors, some acrylic, and artist inks. There's a real history to it. Over the centuries, pirates have added their own secrets and scribbled notes to each other. There're unlimited mysteries held within."

Phrases and text on the map include "Geographic Landmarks and Magic Keys for Spiritual Passage," "Ghosts of Lost Souls at Sea to be Shepherded Through the Watery Passageway," and "Forgotten Sailors Sleep with Eyes Open Dreaming of a Salt Water Death." Poetic locales include the "Sea of Forgotten Loves," "Sea of Weeping Sailors," "Sea of Abandoned Children," "Regretful Beach," "Broken Promise Cove," and "Blue Dream River."

There are also paintings of several creatures, both real and mythological, on the map, including a dragon, a tiger, and a small creature who, curiously, resembles a legendary mouse. When asked about it, Byrkit smiles mischievously and says "There are some secrets on the map that are beyond even *my* understanding!"

Shipwreck City
ANATOMY OF A SCENE

A series of development illustrations, including Gore Verbinski's initial scribble (ABOVE) demonstrates the evolutionary process of Shipwreck City's journey from idea to reality, leading to the actual set built on the Walt Disney Studios Stage 2 (OPPOSITE TOP), which included the three-hundred-foot-long, hand-painted backdrop (OPPOSITE BOTTOM). RIGHT: Illustration by James Ward Byrkit; BELOW AND BOTTOM RIGHT: Illustrations by Nathan Schroeder; BOTTOM LEFT: Illustration by Darek Gogol.

Into The Maelstrom

For the climactic "Maelstrom" sequence of *At World's End*—the massive, apocalyptic battle between the pirate and British East India Company armadas that takes place in a supernaturally induced storm of monumental proportions—the filmmakers had to find a facility in which they could build full-size replicas of both the *Black Pearl* and *Flying Dutchman* from the decks up, as well as various other set pieces. The only such structure anywhere near Los Angeles was Building #703 of the enigmatically named "Site 9." This 600-foot-long, 300-foot-wide, and 70-foot-tall hangar in the desert community of Palmdale, California, north of the Walt Disney Studios in Burbank, was built in 1983 for the assembly of one hundred B-1 bombers, and it had also been used as a shooting stage for a number of other films.

Rick Heinrichs worked in synergistic conjunction with another Academy Award–winner, special effects supervisor John Frazier, to construct the *Pearl* and the *Dutchman*, mounted on massive, highly sophisticated motion bases, surrounded by gigantic blue-screen backings. "This is one of the most elaborate and ambitious action sequences I've ever seen conceived for a film," noted Heinrichs, "and it requires coordination of several departments, including ours, special physical effects, and visual effects. If it's even eighty-five percent of what we hope for, it will be off the charts."

Frazier and his team also designed and built the motion bases for the two "hero" ships. "What we decided to do on *At World's End* that has never been done before on any motion picture," notes Frazier, "was to put a tower at each end of the two ships that allowed us to heave them up fifteen feet. By doing that, we were able to get the actual, realistic movement of a ship in the ocean. We pivoted the ships on each end to bring the bow up and down, and then we had two hydraulic rams on the either side of the ships that allowed them to roll."

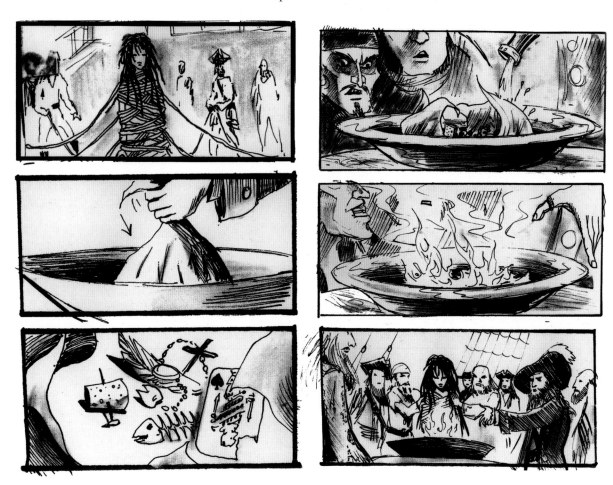

Frazier and his team also designed a system of piping and rain heads that poured hammering showers onto the sets, driven by several gigantic fans capable of blowing winds up to 100 miles per hour. Cinematographer Dariusz Wolski and gaffer Raffi Sanchez then designed a complex grid of 1,400 lights, as well as some 40 lights around the 60-foot-tall blue screen that surrounds the ships.

In the post-production phase, it would be up to John Knoll and his team at ILM to provide the environments, including the turbulent sea and mile-wide whirlpool that threatens any ship that comes too close to its vortex. "Visually, it's a very bold idea," says Knoll, "but there's not really anything you can shoot practically for that. So all the water has to be computer-generated, and it's very difficult to do that realistically. We're going to end up with approximately 400 visual effects shots in that sequence—with rain, giant waves, whitecaps, foam, and spray.

"What's happening in the foreground is pretty complicated as well," Knoll continues. "There's a huge battle between the *Black Pearl* and *Flying Dutchman*, so we have computer-generated characters in the midst of rain, atmospherics, and splintering wood. Not to mention the hundreds of pirate and EITC ships seen in the sequence."

The acoustics in the Site 9 hangar tended to amplify even the sound of a pin dropping, so the collective decibel level of torrents of rain descending from hundreds of spigots, giant fans whirring at propeller speed, cannons roaring from the ships' decks, and special effects mortars loudly blowing debris and small tsunamis of water back *at* the ships—not to mention the cries of pirates and EITC soldiers in combat *on* the ships—was enough to wake the dead, if indeed the dead had been so bold as to approach the location. "Just when we thought we were protected from the elements," noted first assistant director Dave Venghaus, "we created them ourselves."

OPPOSITE: Storyboard sequence in which Barbossa and the *Black Pearl* pirates invoke the sea goddess Calypso's presence; ABOVE: The scene comes to life on film.

BELOW: Filming the Maelstrom sequence with full-sized replicas of both the *Black Pearl* and *Flying Dutchman* mounted on special effects coordinator John Frazier's "tilt rigs"; OPPOSITE TOP: A section of the *Black Pearl* mounted on Frazier's motion base is tested inside the giant Site 9 hangar for the "Green Flash" sequence; OPPOSITE BOTTOM: Stunt players hold on as the *Black Pearl* turns completely upside down.

Gore Verbinski and his crew donned protective gear to allow the water to roll off their backs, as much as possible anyway. The stars and stunt players weren't so fortunate. Keira Knightley recalls: "You're in costume, but you also have a wet suit on underneath. Then they turn the rain on and you're drenched within ten seconds. I feel sorry for the crew because they're in it all day long. The rain is so heavy at times that you literally cannot see. When the *Black Pearl* and *Flying Dutchman* are side-by-side, we're working on a fifteen-percent slope, on which you're running uphill doing a swordfight in torrential rain with an entire camera crew coming at you. It will look great, but it's definitely a hard one to work on."

"We were running away from hurricanes in the Bahamas," adds Johnny Depp, "shooting in Dominica during the rainy season in a rain forest, and then we went to the desert in Palmdale, filming in a downpour and about seventy-five knots of wind inside of a massive facility on a tilted ship.

"Once again, this is one of those situations where it's so weird that you just don't question it anymore. 'Johnny, we're going to drive you an hour and a half up to the desert, you're going to climb aboard the *Black Pearl* and *Flying Dutch-man* built on gigantic rigs, and we're going to buffet you with high winds and rain while you sword fight at a steep angle.'

"And you just kind of go, 'Okay, fine. No problem.'"

The Beauty of Coincidence

It took a tough technical team to survive the challenges of the three Pirates films. Director of Photography Dariusz (Darek) Wolski and his team—including key grip Mike (Pop) Popovich; chief lighting technician Rafael (Raffi) Sanchez; camera operators/assistants Martin Schaer, David Luckenbach, Trevor Loomis, James Goldman, Nino Neuboeck, Chris Garcia, and Rodney Sandoral; underwater unit head Pete Zuccarini; and aerial unit head David B. Nowell—faced every test thrown at them with incomparable energy and true grit.

"Darek is a brilliant artist," states Jerry Bruckheimer. "I've worked with him a number of times. He's very quick, gets things done, and does very complex lighting in a minimal amount of time."

"Once you accept that you don't have complete control over the elements, you can get creative," explains Wolski. "When you're dealing with forces of nature—the sun going in different directions, clouds coming in, wind blowing, you have to be flexible and often come up with an idea at the last minute. There's so much beauty in coincidence. I don't believe in rules. I believe in intuition. No matter how many discussions, storyboards, or pre-visualizations were created, we had to adapt constantly."

Richard Jones, a member of Mike Popovich's grip department, designed and built a complex camera platform utilized for the second two films, which was mounted on a construction crane and capable of holding an entire Super Technocrane. The unit stood as tall as the highest masts of the ships, giving Verbinski and Wolski freedom to film the Kraken attacks or Maelstrom from extremely high angles by employing a remote-control camera at the end of the Technocrane. "We've shot pretty much every possible situation," notes Wolski. "In jungles, water, under water, dark holes, on bright salt flats, on soundstages. At one point, Jerry Bruckheimer said, with his typical understatement, 'It's pretty big, isn't it?' I replied, 'Yeah, it's all downhill now.' And Jerry said, with a grin on his face, 'That's what they told me when I did *Beverly Hills Cop.*'"

BELOW: Director of photography Dariusz Wolski up to his waist in water on the Pantano River set at the Walt Disney Studios; OPPOSITE TOP: Underwater photography near the *Interceptor* (portrayed by the *Lady Washington*); OPPOSITE BOTTOM: Underwater director of photography Pete Zuccarini (left) literally working side-by-side in the briny deep with Dariusz Wolski.

Costumes
RAGS TO RICHES

Throughout the filming of the three Pirates of the Caribbean films, costume designer Penny Rose was also a master builder—only using fabrics, rather than bricks and mortar—with a passionate attention to detail. The indomitable Rose designed every single costume, whether it was for one of the stars or an extra who played the sixth pirate from the left. Notes Lee Arenberg, who portrays the pirate Pintel, "Penny is amazing because she'll have a pile of clothes sitting there, and with her keen eye she'll pick a garment out, have it distressed, aged, dyed, and suddenly, it becomes more than a costume. It becomes your character."

"Penny Rose is a force of nature," says Tom Hollander (Lord Cutler Beckett). "She's a very important person on the film, with boundless energy. In her wardrobe warehouse, Penny is like an empress in a tent of fabrics, with a lot of assistants rushing around, bringing this and that. 'No, the brocade. No, the gold. Bring the blue. I'm sick of the red. No, take it out. Bring it back. Take it in. Pull it down.'"

For *The Curse of the Black Pearl*, Rose was nominated for both the British Academy of Film and Television Arts (BAFTA) and Costume Designers Guild awards. In between *The Curse of the Black Pearl* and *Dead Man's Chest*, Rose worked with Keira Knightley on the Jerry Bruckheimer Films production of *King Arthur*.

Rose and her department literally combed the world for fabrics and materials from which to create the thousands of costumes required, all designed with the aid of associate costume designer John Norster, costume supervisor Kenny Crouch (both of whom she refers to as "the most important men in my life"), and a large staff of costumers, cutters, agers, dyers, buyers, painters, leathermakers, and various assistants. Of paramount importance to Rose was for the costumes to look as if they were created in the eighteenth century in every detail. "I only do *real*," says Rose. "When I first met Gore, I told him 'I might lose this job, but the truth is I can't do costumes. I just dress people. If you want to do it filthy and real, I'd love to have a go. If you want to do mini-opera, you can probably get somebody else.' But filthy and real was *exactly* what Gore wanted!

"There's a lot of fantasy in the story, but not in the costumes," Rose continues. "We want these clothes to look like they've been slept in and worn forever. Aging and dying costumes for a period film is absolutely vital. I don't like people to look as if they've just walked out of a shop. It's a really specialized field, very underestimated and undervalued, and the people who do it are geniuses because it's very subtle. For example, all of the shoes go into a cement mixer with a few rocks and by the time they come out, they've aged five years."

"I don't consider that I design a costume and then superimpose it upon somebody," notes Rose. "It's definitely a duet." The "Jack Sparrow" look has already become a classic example of helping to

OPPOSITE, LEFT, and BELOW RIGHT: Detailed sketches of costumes for Elizabeth Swann, Jack Sparrow, and Governor Weatherby Swann by Darrell Warner for designer Penny Rose, BELOW LEFT.

create a character by making certain that he's in the right togs. "When Johnny came in for his first fitting,' explains Rose, "I had a few ready-made pieces to try some shapes on. Once I put that hat on his head, he was sold. I hadn't even made it especially for him, it was part of some samples, but Johnny said 'I'm not parting with the hat.' So if I'm honest about it, I think we started from the hat downwards, and since Captain Jack is a rock and roll pirate, it just evolved from Johnny feeling comfortable in something and not departing from it."

Captain Jack Sparrow's now-famous look was a collaboration in the first film between Penny Rose, makeup designer Ve Neill, key hair designer Martin Samuel, and Depp himself. "Having spent some time with Keith Richards was certainly a huge part of the inspiration for the character," says the actor. "I spent a little time with Keith here and there, and each time I'd see him he'd have a new thing tied into his hair. 'What is that hanging?,' I'd ask, and Keith would say 'Ah yeah, I got that in Bermuda,' or wherever. So it felt to me like Jack, on his travels and adventures, would see something and go 'Oh yeah, I'll keep that,' tie it in his hair or have someone else do it. Each little trinket would have a story. For example, the bone that hangs just above the bandana is a shinbone from a reindeer. Then Jack has the dangly bits, beads, a chicken foot, a fertility symbol, weird animal tails. There's no telling where he got those, and it might have been lunch!"

For *Dead Man's Chest* and *At World's End*, "Johnny's added a few things this time," Rose notes. "He's a very thoughtful, caring actor in terms of how he looks in character."

Will Turner, as played by Orlando Bloom, undergoes a dramatic progression of character from one film to the next, and his costumes needed to reflect that journey. "In the first film, Will Turner was a blacksmith with a crush on the governor's daughter. In *Dead Man's Chest*, he's matured and has a more exciting look," explains Rose. "Orlando and I got together and had a bit of a back-and-forth, and I thought we would make Will look a little more sophisticated. For a good deal of the film, he's wearing an olive-green leather pirate coat that makes him look more powerful."

Says Bloom, "Penny has done an amazing job of taking Will to another level and loosening him up. The leather coat we chose for Will to wear is kind of like a biker jacket for pirate times. Doing sword fights and getting wet in a long leather coat has posed a few challenges, to say the least, but it's worth every moment because Penny's vision for Will, and all of the characters, has helped them come alive." Bloom's main costume, it might be added, includes a cream embroidered waistcoat that Rose constructed using antique table linens found in Paris, a perfect example of her determination to use whatever is necessary to accomplish her design goals.

The casting of Keira Knightley as Elizabeth Swann in *The Curse of the Black Pearl* presented Penny Rose with all sorts of possibilities for her adornments. "Keira was a dream to dress, because she is

TOP: Costumer Scott R. Hankins fixes Geoffrey Rush's costume; BOTTOM: Costume sketch for Captain Jack by Darrell Warner.

young, enthusiastic, and would stand still for eight hours," recalls Rose. "The first thing you see her in is the dress that her father, Governor Weatherby Swann, has bought her. The idea was that the dress was made in London, very lavish, with her father trying to give his daughter a little bit of European sophistication. Yet you have to be very careful with a seventeen-year-old actress that you don't end up with the dress wearing her instead of the other way around. Gore kept saying that for Elizabeth it should be a 'golden' moment, so I just went for golden fabric. I found reproduction eighteenth-century material, a silk taffeta that's so light that when it's made it doesn't feel enormous. I think the overall effect is that while this is something that a father might wish for his daughter to wear, it's not necessarily what a daughter would particularly choose.

"Keira has several different looks in *Dead Man's Chest*," Rose continues, "because Elizabeth is really changing and maturing as well. Keira really took to the boy's clothing that she wears for part of the film. She also wears a beautiful wedding gown, but we only see it drenched in rain!"

"Having worked with Penny on Pirates and *King Arthur*, I feel like I've spent my life with her, and I love it," says Knightley. "She is, in the best possible way, a perfectionist. One of my favorite parts of filming is before we even start, when I have costume fittings with Penny. I see her in charge of hundreds and hundreds of costumes, yet, as soon as you get into her fitting room, she just cuts right to it. If you've got a button that's two millimeters out of place, Penny will move it. If something needs a bit of embroidery to be brought out, she sees it immediately. She's a forceful lady, and one that I'm very glad to have around."

ABOVE: Jack Sparrow's dreads and threads in *Dead Man's Chest.*

143

Elizabeth's wedding gown is a fine example of Penny Rose's minute attention to detail. It is comprised of a deep ivory silk and raffia fabric embellished with a leaf, floral, and fan design. Rose used the fabric "as is" for the skirts, but created her own design on the bodice by cutting around and repositioning the raffia details. The stomacher (front of the dress) looks almost embroidered, with layer upon layer of this raffia design sewn into it. The veil is an ivory silk chiffon, with delicate pearls sewn into the silk, attached to a wired tiara that also contains the raffia fabric from the dress. The petticoat was actually constructed from an antique quilted cotton bedspread from Rome.

Some of the new characters in *Dead Man's Chest* and *At World's End* also enticed Rose to new heights of creativity. "I loved doing Tia Dalma's attire, which was difficult, because the character lives in a swamp and she's both glamorous and repulsive at the same time. You wouldn't want to sit too close to her, yet we still want to feel her power as a woman. I thoroughly enjoyed creating for, as well as working with, the lovely Naomie Harris."

"I absolutely love everything about how they've created Tia Dalma," enthuses Harris, who is unrecognizable in her full makeup, hair, and costume. "Penny's costumes, the makeup that Ve Neill designed, the hair by Martin Samuel—I think it's all absolutely fabulous. I didn't recognize myself at all when I looked in the mirror, and that's the way it should be. I love the fact that Tia Dalma is such a rugged, earthy, crazy kind of character, because I've never played anything like this before."

Although the physical details of Bill Nighy's Davy Jones would be created through computer generated imagery, Rose nonetheless created an actual costume that served as a model for the ILM artists to work from. "They photographed Bill in his costume in minute detail, because you can't just superimpose a concept onto a gray reference suit," she says.

Synergy was key to the evolution of the creative elements of the Pirates films, and Rose always worked in concert with production designers Brian Morris (*The Curse of the Black Pearl*) and Rick Heinrichs (*Dead Man's Chest* and *At World's End*), Ve Neill, Martin Samuel, and others to ensure that her pieces fit into the overall puzzle. Splendid examples of this were the colorful and sometimes outlandish designs that defined the human-munching Pelegostos in *Dead Man's Chest*. Heinrichs, of course, designed their physical environment, with Rose contributing adornments, including body paint (a kind of costume that isn't really a costume). And Ve Neill's and Martin Samuel's makeup and hair departments provided the artistry required to bring the concepts into reality.

Clothes Make the Man (and Woman)

In *At World's End*, the story and character developments go hand-in-hand with their costume changes. "We see a more confident and powerful Will Turner and a new and exciting Elizabeth Swann," states Rose. "We've given Orlando an embossed buckskin vest, a dark, wine-colored shirt, and a beautiful, mud cloth coat. I think it's important that in the third film, you're slightly confused as to whose side Will is on, so we needed to help his character look a little bit darker, metaphorically.

"Keira gets to wear a Chinese courtesan costume, with a heavily jeweled and ornate headdress and matching collar piece, a tasseled vest, and an embroidered silk gown with what would probably have been a skirt, but which, for practical reasons, we turned into culottes so that when she gets to the fighting sequences, we could lose the vest and the other accessories and go straight into action mode."

Rose also designed an astonishing costume for Captain Sao Feng. "Chow Yun-Fat is the Laurence Olivier of the East, and it took less than ten minutes of the fitting to see that this fellow really knows his stuff," says Rose. "Yun-Fat knows how to envelop himself in the character. He knew we were here to give him the visual, and he did everything possible to help us. It quickly evolved into a joint decision-making process about what's happening in that mirror, then how we could progress and make it a bigger and better work. Chow Yun-Fat already has a powerful presence in person, but we needed this Chinese pirate captain to be *terrifying*."

Rose also had an opportunity to design a costume for Bill Nighy in a flashback scene in which the audience can see what Davy Jones looked like as a man "before he was under the sea for years and years and barnacled up. We finally get Bill out of those gray CGI reference pajamas, for which he's very, very grateful," she says with a laugh.

For *At World's End*, Rose also designed costumes for buccaneers from all corners of the globe: Africa, the Middle East, Asia, Europe, and the Americas. Primary among this group are the Pirate Lords who convene in Shipwreck City, and chief among them is the Keeper of the Code, Captain Teague, played by Keith Richards. "I was fortunate enough to give Mr. Richards a fitting in July 2005, when he was in Los Angeles just prior to band rehearsals," recalls Rose. "It was a week when Johnny Depp was not working, but I asked him to come with me, which he very kindly did. I must say, it was fairly hilarious to see the two of them together, because once Keith was dressed in costume, you really could believe that the two of them were related.

"It was a bizarre moment," continues Rose, "because how often do you get to costume a rock icon? (Well, actually, Rose has done it before for Bob Geldof in *Pink Floyd: The Wall*, and Madonna in *Evita*). But Keith was *dying* to be a pirate. I mean, he wanted to go out that night dressed in the pirate costume! So I think he really enjoyed the process."

OPPOSITE TOP: Crew members attend to Geoffrey Rush, Keira Knightley, and Johnny Depp for the *At World's End* Parlay sequence; OPPOSITE BOTTOM: Sketch by Darrell Warner of Elizabeth Swann when she impersonates a male sailor; LEFT: Costumes were often drenched by man-made rain; ABOVE: Chow Yun-Fat's costume for Captain Sao Feng weighed more than twenty pounds, but he said it was worth each one of them.

Hair & Makeup
THE BAD AND THE BEAUTIFUL

Makeup effects creator and department head Ve Neill and chief hairstylist Martin Samuel do wonderful and terrible things to people. They take perfectly reasonable looking human beings, lure them into their air-conditioned trailers and when they emerge again in anywhere from ten minutes to five hours, they are utterly, completely, and often amazingly, transformed.

For their efforts on *The Curse of the Black Pearl*, Neill and Samuel were both honored with Academy Award nominations in the Best Makeup category. For the Pirates films, Neill and Samuel stretched their considerable talents to the fullest, and their respective departments—huge by any cinematic standards—were comprised of some of the industry's most talented and experienced artists. Working with Ve Neill were key makeup artist Joel Harlow, additional supervisor Ken Diaz, and twenty-six additional artists, among them the brilliant veteran Richard Snell, who tragically passed away just before the film completed filming on location in the Caribbean. Working with Martin Samuel and key hairstylist Lucia Mace were yet another twenty-six gifted experts, combing, teasing, and curling to a fare-thee-well. Neill and Samuel were integral to the character-building process, from Captain Jack Sparrow and the other leading players to indescribably filthy, scabby, and scarred pirates of the world and from elaborately body-painted, quasi-comical cannibals to powdered and wigged eighteenth-century British dandies to toothsome Tortuga wenches.

Neill and Samuel both made indelible contributions to the look of Johnny Depp's Captain Jack. "Johnny is very clever and he has very quirky ideas," says Neill, who had previously worked with the actor on *Edward Scissorhands*,

OPPOSITE: Actors as brilliantly and bizarrely dressed Pelegostos tribesmen; ABOVE: Academy Award–winning Ve Neill puts some finishing touches on Chow Yun-Fat's brow.

Blow, and *Ed Wood*, for which she won her third of three Oscars. "Anything goes with Johnny, and anything to make the character that much groovier. We didn't want him to look as grimy as the other pirates, so we used a stipple form on him, done by a repeated tapping of the brush, which gives him a little bit more of a ruddy look. As for the black around his eyes, it's not mascara, as some believe."

"Berbers used to wear kohl under their eyes for protection in the desert," says Depp. "So I figured that for a guy being out at sea, it would almost be like modern-day football players who use the stuff for protection from sun reflection."

"They didn't have sunglasses in the eighteenth century," adds Neill, "and if you look through old books and prints you'll see that pirates had black grease, charcoal, or soot beneath their eyes to protect them from the glare of the sun and the ocean."

"As for the gold and silver teeth," Depp adds, "that's sort of mathematics. With pirates, you expect it. I originally had more, but the studio wasn't particularly enthused with them, so I cut back a little."

Regarding the good captain's dreadlocks, Martin Samuel recalls that "Johnny had some things in mind that he spoke to Gore about, including his desire for beads and coins attached to his long hair. Most actors preconceive the look that they think they would like. Sometimes they're right and sometimes they're very wrong and you have to guide them away. But in this case, Johnny's ideas were great. So I put a test wig together, and both Johnny and Gore loved it. The first makeup and hair tests for Johnny were very successful."

In the hair and makeup trailers, the Jack Sparrow wig took on something of an aura of being a holy relic, to be approached with respect, even awe. Martin Samuel took something of a less orthodox approach, however, affectionately referring to it as "Mrs. Wiggins."

To make the films' vast array of pirates look as gnarly as possible, Neill relied on innovative makeup techniques. "We layer the color with a brush, rather than smudge it on with a sponge," she notes. "That way it gets into the creases and make the pirates look really gritty and grimy. Then you layer other colors on top of it, so they start looking sunburned and filthy. Some of them have salt sores on their face or peeling sunburns. We also use a lot of contact lenses to make their eyes yellow and rheumy looking." As for that parade of discolored, decaying, and rather disgusting teeth, "We use a simple little colored plastic vacuum form that slides over their teeth so we never have to worry about touching up the teeth or making rotten false ones. It works really well because it's comfortable for the actors and doesn't impair their speech." For the cadres of extras, Neill and company did use a technique of painting disturbingly realistic discoloration directly onto their teeth, which thankfully could be removed at the end of a workday.

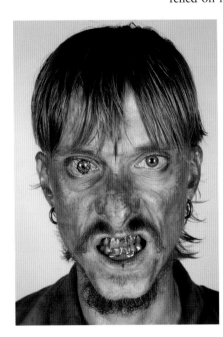

Under Neill's supervision, hundreds of pairs of contact lenses were created for the three films by Professional Visioncare Associates. "We made lenses for nearly all of the principal actors, most of the Pelegostos, and many of the stuntmen," explains contact lens coordinator Cristina P. Ceret. "They were nearly all soft lenses of varying types

TOP LEFT: Captain Jack Sparrow's legendary look; LEFT: Mackenzie Crook wore two contact lenses to give the impression of a wooden eye and accessories to make his teeth look suitably rotten.

148

and designs. The Pelegostos had hand-painted soft scleral lenses to give them a scarred/bloodshot effect. Many of the pirates wore hand-painted soft lenses to provide a jaundiced effect, and Tia Dalma had an extreme bloodshot effect. Designs were changed a few times until Ve Neill, Joel Harlow, and Gore Verbinski were satisfied."

Ragetti's wooden eye became a character almost unto itself throughout the three films. Actor Mackenzie Crook has to wear not one, but two, contact lenses for this effect, wearing both soft and hard scleral lenses, one on top of the other. "It's uncomfortable," he admitted, "but not painful. And it helps the character, because without it, I'm just any other pirate."

ABOVE: Key makeup artist and makeup effects supervisor Joel Harlow attends to Stellan Skarsgård's astonishing appliances.

ABOVE: Chief hairstylist Martin Samuel attends to Keira Knightley in the Singapore bathhouse set; BELOW: Personnel attend to Tom Hollander's wig.

Stunts
HANGING FROM THE RAFTERS

Although George Marshall Ruge, a man who's coordinated some of the most innovative, elegant, and sublimely spectacular stunts in recent movie history, is uncommonly soft-spoken, the action scenes that he's coordinated in all The Lord of the Rings and Pirates of the Caribbean films speak very loudly for his, and his vast department's, talent. From innovative sword fights to meticulously choreographed and hugely elaborate pieces of action-comedy business, Ruge, assistant stunt coordinator Dan Barringer, and their entire team unleashed the deepest depths of their creativity and emerged as true screen heroes.

Ruge's work for *The Curse of the Black Pearl* included classic ship-to-ship battles and some killer sword fighting sequences, including the acrobatic matchup between Captain Jack Sparrow and Will Turner in the Port Royal blacksmith's shed and the climactic clash between Sparrow and Captain Barbossa in the treasure cave.

Born in San Francisco, Ruge studied theater arts and acting at San Francisco State University, where he also studied fencing, specializing in the saber. Since then, he has dueled on stage and screen. "I might differ a little from other stunt coordinators," Ruge confesses, "in that I approach the work from the inside out. I don't ever want stunts to be about the 'gag.' That's just part of what's happening to tell the story, and our ultimate obligation is to help in that regard and not show off. If a stunt occurs in the upper left hand corner of the screen, that's fine with me."

Ruge was first attracted to Pirates of the Caribbean by what he calls "the epic value." "It brought to me visions of the kind of wide-screen movies from the 1940s and 1950s that we so love. I was looking for something like that, a project with big scope and huge scale. Knowing that Jerry Bruckheimer was producing it sealed it for me. Jerry is legendary, and I figured that if this was his project, I had to be onboard." Ruge was also delighted by his first meetings with Gore Verbinski. "I had expected I'd have to go in there and do a lot of talking, but instead I

OPPOSITE: In *At World's End*, pirates escape from the *Flying Dutchman* on lines connected to the *Empress*, which is being towed behind it; ABOVE: Captain Jack Sparrow and Will Turner cross swords in a blacksmith's work-shop in *The Curse of the Black Pearl*.

got excited and inspired by Gore's vision of the project. He has the energy of a little kid, and he's very visual. I knew right away that we would connect."

Ruge was delighted to reunite with so many of the same personnel from *The Curse of the Black Pearl*, particularly the stars. "Johnny's a natural who doesn't let on that it comes so easily to him," he says. "He's a very good athlete who colors all of the action with character. *Dead Man's Chest* and *At World's End* are my fifth and sixth films with Orlando, and they've all been big action movies. He's also a fantastic athlete, and loves performing action. I keep telling Keira that if it ever falls apart for her, we'll give her a T-shirt and a hat, and bring her on the stunt team. Her physicality is fantastic."

Dead Man's Chest and *At World's End* presented Ruge with even greater challenges than *The Curse of the Black Pearl*. The first major stunt sequence for *Dead Man's Chest* was in a large Tortuga tavern designed and built on the Universal Studios backlot, where Captain Jack and Joshamee Gibbs search for a crew of souls to man the *Flying Dutchman*. This sequence culminates in a boisterous brawl carefully choreographed by Ruge that provided the physically fearless Keira

ABOVE: Filming the incredibly complex runaway mill-wheel sequence in a thick coconut grove in Hampstead, Dominica.

Knightley with her first of many opportunities to shine. "I had about two weeks training for that in an L.A. studio," recalls Knightley. "When we actually came to shoot it, it was slightly different because, rather than an open studio, we were in a location just crammed full of people, and it was a night shoot as well. I didn't get to do my bit until about four in the morning, which isn't really the best way to do a fight sequence. I just drank *a lot* of coffee."

"Keira is a real quick study," confirms Ruge, "and a true athlete. We're pretty jaded in this business, but the crew was pretty amazed at what Keira accomplished. When you get applause like that on set, it's a good sign."

One of the most imaginative and expansive stunt sequences in *Dead Man's Chest* is the now-famous three-way sword fight between Captain Jack Sparrow, Will Turner, and James Norrington on the runaway mill wheel, which was filmed both in Dominica and The Exumas, difficult locations all. "The wheel was a very difficult set piece for all concerned," explains Ruge. "There were extreme physical demands and a number of safety concerns involved." The mill-wheel sequence is a perfect example of the synergy between departments that characterized the entire production. Recalls Ruge, "Many departments and people were involved in making the wheel sequence a reality. I specifically worked in collaboration with the special effects and visual effects coordinators, production designer, art director, propmaster, construction coordinator, director of photography, camera operators, and more. But most notably it was Gore's grand vision, commitment, and enthusiasm that inspired the sequence for all of us. I worked closely with him in every aspect to help bring it to life."

There were two versions of the wheel—one a "cart" version supported by "training wheels" pulled by cables on a winch system, with camera platforms built onto the training wheel cart that surrounded it. "The other version," notes Ruge, "was affectionately called the 'paint roller.' The wheel was attached to steel tow bars and literally towed by a flatbed truck that also served as a makeshift camera platform at times." To enable the wheel to roll more smoothly, paths were created through the jungle, because if the terrain was too tough, "it made it impossible for the performers to stay on the wheel, or maintain the necessary hand/eye coordination for the sword fight."

Before the sequence went in front of the cameras, there were several pre-production rehearsals within a five week span, and a series of location rehearsals over the course of three weeks whenever time permitted Ruge to muster the three actors and his stunt team.

LEFT: Stunt double Tony Angelotti, arrayed as Captain Jack, in the mill-wheel sequence; ABOVE: Stunt coordinator George Marshall Ruge (back to camera) advises Orlando Bloom while the actor ascends the mill wheel.

"Oh, boy, I'll never forget the faces on Gore and George when it was time to load me into that massive wheel," recalls Johnny Depp. "Gore just started laughing, because it was such an absurd and bizarre request for grown men to ask of each other: 'Okay, what we'd like to do now is bind you inside the wheel, tether you to the walls of this thing, give you a sword, and as the wheel is rolling you're gonna go upside down several times.'

"It was so bizarre that it was completely appealing," Depp continues. "I've done some really obtuse and strange things in this movie—at some point there are no surprises. But because of who Gore and George are and how brilliant they are at their jobs, you have complete trust, which is the whole key to filmmaking."

"It's a truly remarkable sequence that only Gore, Ted, and Terry could have come up with, and that only George could have made work," says Orlando Bloom. "We spent many days harnessed inside of that wheel, doing crazy fights up and down, around and around. It would make a fun ride in an amusement park, if it weren't so uncomfortable." Also occasionally harnessed inside of the wheel doing 360-degree revolutions were camera operators Martin Schaer and Josh Bleibtreu.

While filming the three-way sword fight, Verbinski and company found themselves in a thick grove of coconut palms, which wouldn't have been so daunting if heavy coconuts hadn't been occasionally falling from heights of nearly one hundred feet. Everyone in the thick of the action had to wear hard hats. Verbinski donned an old-fashioned pith helmet.

Jack Davenport points out that although there are CGI elements that enhance the scene, most of it live on-camera. "It's a classic sword fight scene with shots that can't be faked. When you see us upside down with the veins in our forehead popping out, it's real."

But the boys weren't the only ones who got to have fun. Sequences shot in Dominica and The Exumas also gave Keira Knightley ample opportunity to flex her action muscles, and the fearless performer was up for anything Ruge wanted to throw at her. The climax of *Dead Man's Chest* called upon Knightley to take two swords in hand and kick some serious *Flying Dutchman*–crewmen butt. "The weather was absolutely boiling, and we were in this amazing coconut grove," she recalls. "George and his stunt team were completely fantastic. They're so patient and really take you through the action one step at a time. I'm a huge believer that if this is something that my character has got to do, then I want to really know how to do it. And if you're shooting an action movie, it's really boring if you don't actually do the action. When you're doing the fight sequences, a lot of the time we're having a full run at it, so you can really get into it, and that's fantastic. It's nice to feel like you're a part of the team. What George and his people do is invite you into the team. And my stunt double, Lisa Hoyle, is absolutely brilliant."

RIGHT: Keira Knightley gets her wish to sword fight; OPPOSITE: Filming the Bone Cage scene in Dominica.

The other stunt doubles for the stars in all three Pirates films were equally brilliant. They included Tony Angelotti, Theo Kypri, Zach Hudson, and Thomas Dupont, who leapt and fought, and achieved truly death-defying feats when common sense (and insurance policies) prevented an often willing Depp, Bloom, and Knightley from accomplishing the stunts themselves.

Bones, Beaches, and Kraken Attacks

A section of the Pelegostos village sequence, in which Will Turner and other *Black Pearl* pirates are imprisoned in large circular cages made of human bones (actually fabricated from latex and foam), was shot in Dominica's TiTou Gorge, part of the magnificent Morne Trois Pitons National Park in Dominica's south-central interior. Icy waters necessitated the crew donning wet suits. "Just when I was thinking, in sizzling hot Dominica, that I had forgotten what it was like to be cold, Pirates of the Caribbean granted my wish," says Kevin R. McNally. "For the scene in which the bone cage drops into a gorge, they found the coldest water in Dominica and kept us there for two days!"

The bone-cage scene was another event that required the expertise of a whole range of departments, including, of course, Ruge's. "The reality of putting people into these things, rolling them down hills, off cliffs, and swinging between cliff walls proved extremely problematic," he says. "How do you build a cage that's structurally sound but light enough for people to pick up and run with? There was a lot of research and development, and we came up with various versions of the cage. One was made of lightweight foam to run with and another was built from more substantial materials for rolling. It was pretty difficult to navigate with six people and twelve legs sticking out of this thing," he adds.

Verbinski continued directing the Pelegostos bone-cage sequence in Palos Verdes, California, and this time, some of the actors—including Orlando Bloom, Kevin R. McNally, David Bailie, and Martin Klebba—found themselves in a cage suddenly suspended from a one-hundred-foot-tall crane, swinging freely in long, wide arcs. Bloom definitely enjoyed the ride, while others looked more than a little green in the gills.

"The bone-cage sequence was crazy," Bloom recalls. "The first time we dropped from the crane, nobody knew what to expect, and it was like a bungee-jump feeling. Your stomach completely leaves you. Believe me, moments like that will never be forgotten!"

And then there was Captain Jack Sparrow's mad dash down the beach to escape from a highly agitated group of islanders, filmed on Dominica's Hampstead Beach. "It was utterly exhausting," admits Johnny Depp.

155

"Two hundred people dressed as natives chasing me down the shoreline on the beach while I'm in full Jack Sparrow regalia. It felt like days and days of that. But the end result was worth it."

For the Kraken attacks on both the *Edinburgh Trader* and *Black Pearl*, Ruge and his team of stunt players and riggers had to create multiple ratchets to simulate people getting whacked or pulled into the air by the monster's tentacles. "The reality of doing the stunt rigging on these ships is that there's a mast here, or ropes hanging down there, or grates in the middle of the deck," he notes. "So we built an overhead system on both of the ships that ran their full lengths in between the yardarms, with travelers on the cables that allowed us to move with pinpoint accuracy to virtually anywhere in between the masts. We were on water, so everything was moving, but the multi-layered system gave us the ability to move things around pretty freely."

Among the stunt heroes for these sequences was Orlando Bloom himself, who as often as feasible (and as permitted by production) performed his own spectacular feats of derring-do, including one more than thirty feet up in the rigging of the *Edinburgh Trader*. "There's one scene in which I'm on the mast, jump into a sail, slash it with a dagger and slide down." says Bloom. "This is real Errol Flynn, which is every boy's dream. But I've trained hard to be fit and agile enough to do things like this so I don't hurt myself. It's a major part of who Will Turner is."

ABOVE: An action-packed battle breaks out on the docks of Singapore between Chinese pirates and soldiers from the East India Trading Company; RIGHT: Ragetti and Pintel attempt to spirit away the priceless Dead Man's Chest.

Over the Edge Action

At *World's End* presented new and occasionally overwhelming challenges to George Marshall Ruge and company. The film opens with an elaborate action sequence involving Captain Barbossa, Will Turner, Elizabeth Swann, Gibbs, Tia Dalma, Pintel and Ragetti, Cotton and his parrot, Marty, Captain Sao Feng,

"Jack" the Monkey, and approximately 200 assorted Chinese pirates, East India Trading Company militia, and various Singaporean citizenry, as all these personnel spill out from a grotty bathhouse onto the streets and alleys of the city, then onto wooden boardwalks and walkways connecting thatched stilt houses over the harbor. "The Singapore sequence began as a one-line description in a treatment," notes Ruge. "Without a lot of warning it took on massive proportions, with a rapid evolution into a complex sequence on a very difficult set. We had limited time to prepare, design the action, choreograph, and rehearse. Because the sets were still being built and the paint was still drying, I ended up calling rehearsals at very odd hours that often extended into the night."

"The bathhouse portion of the sequence presented a lot of problems," Ruge continues. "Complex fight choreography was required in a very confined space with lots of people and lots of obstacles in terms of the baths themselves. The set was raked and incredibly slippery, with the steam rising from all crevices. The action was designed to be absolutely character driven, fresh, intricate, and crisp. There was literally no room for error with gunfire and swords flying everywhere. Once the action leaves the bathhouse and escalates out onto the streets of Singapore, another set of problems emerge. The action had to utilize the very narrow wood-planked walkways that were elevated above the water by bamboo scaffolding. This required performers taking eight- to fourteen-foot falls into the water, which was only three and one half feet deep with a concrete bottom."

Ruge's solution was to sink large sections of black foam rubber and anchor them to the soundstage floor. The problem is that foam rubber's natural inclination is to float, so holes needed to be cut throughout the foam to allow the water to pool above the submerged pad and hold it down.

Late winter weather on Grand Bahama Island also kicked up the seas considerably, as Verbinski and the company learned the hard way while attempting to shoot an *At World's End* sequence in which Elizabeth Swann and some Chinese pirates escape imprisonment on the *Flying Dutchman* by crawling along a tow rope connecting that ship to the *Empress*—Captain Sao Feng's flagship junk. A stiff wind whipped the waters into a whirlpool, with the *Dutchman* and the *Empress* tossed about like toys, and the smaller support craft even more so. "That night was surreal," recalls Ruge. "The stuntmen had to negotiate a 150-foot-long line, hand-over-hand, while alternating their leg holds on the rope as they went. The physical demands were already extreme, but what we didn't

ABOVE: Preparing to film stunt players crawling on the lines between the *Flying Dutchman* and the *Empress* in Grand Bahama Island; BELOW: Stunt coordinator George Marshall Ruge (in visor) surrounded by members of his stunt team.

anticipate was bad weather and rough seas. We're not talking just rolling waves, we're talking about a churning cauldron of wickedly, unpredictably rough water. The seas became too rough for the pick-up boats to navigate, the rope itself was heaving up and down as much as ten feet. Conditions couldn't have been worse. We ended up using another vessel that had a roof to get the stuntmen off the rope. The roof had to be reinforced, as it wasn't mean to carry the weight of people on top. The stuntmen had to time their transfer from the heaving rope to spotters on the boat's roof. The real stunts were performed behind-the-scenes that night!"

As the incredibly brave stunt players crawled along the rope, executive producer Eric McLeod noted, "Take a good look at this. You'll never see moviemaking on this scale again. Soon it'll all be done with blue screen. This is movie history being made."

"The Maelstrom climax was the most spectacular and challenging for us on *At World's End*," notes Ruge. "All of the principal cast were involved, and there were multiple story lines being played out within the epic action." For this massive final ship-to-ship showdown between the pirates and the East India Trading Company, Ruge coordinated stunt sequences both in The Bahamas and inside of the massive Site 9 hangar used for shooting in Palmdale, California. "Because the ship set pieces on Grand Bahama were not particularly designed for stunt rigging opportunities, we had to be very creative to pull off the action," says Ruge. "These ships and the pirates on them take heavy cannon fire. We used multiple air ramps, and wire and ratchet work to create the illusion of our stunt pirates taking this fire. And because these were floating set pieces, we had the luxury of performing the action all the way from the decks and masts to the water in many instances.

"Inside of the Palmdale stage," Ruge concludes, "we at least had the luxury of being indoors and not having to worry about the elements, but we faced a whole new set of challenges because of the immense number of visual and physical effects required for the sequence. Just when we thought we were finally out of hot water, it went way beyond the boiling point in terms of action!"

BELOW: Man-made torrential rain and wind present tough conditions for actors and stunt players in the Maelstrom sequence for *At World's End*; OPPOSITE: Captain Jack takes possession of the Dead Man's Chest.

Visual and Special Effects
MAKING THE UNREAL REAL

J ust another tool in the toolbox," Gore Verbinski says of visual effects. That is an interesting comment from a man who has not only consistently made extensive use of such magic, but has at every available opportunity instigated quantum leaps in the technology. But Verbinski strongly sees visual effects as a means of embellishing and enhancing what's already established in story and character, never for their own sake.

Verbinski and Jerry Bruckheimer knew that the right toolboxes were at Industrial Light & Magic, George Lucas's legendary Northern California facility. Leading the ILM team for all three films was three-time Academy Award nominee (including a nomination for *The Curse of the Black Pearl*) visual effects supervisor John Knoll. Bill George and Roger Guyett functioned as additional supervisors on the second and third films, with Ned Gorman and Jill Brooks handling visual effects–producing chores; Hal Hickel supervising the extensive amount of animation; and visual effects art director Aaron McBride and an army of computer graphics, digital compositing, CG animation, and Sabre artists laboring morning, noon, night, and morning again to make the impossible possible. Also working on visual effects was Charles Gibson, a longtime member of Gore Verbinski's key creative team, who also worked with the director on *Mouse Hunt*, *The Ring*, and *The Weather Man*.

Despite the fact that the film traffics in pure fantasy, Verbinski was absolutely insistent that the unbelievable look believable in every way. "Because Gore has been through the process and understands every nut and bolt of what ILM is doing," says Charlie Gibson, "he can put that aside and just charge forward, knowing that ILM will eventually be able to catch up and meet his vision somewhere near the end of the schedule. What's unique about the visual effects in these films is how freely Gore is able to use what ILM can offer. The net result of that confidence and understanding is that the discussions move on past the technical to the creative."

For each of the Pirates films, Verbinski and Bruckheimer sought to raise the bar a little higher in terms of creating what had never been seen before in the world of visual effects. "The first time Audio-Animatronics were used in the Disney Pirates attraction," said the director, "seeing the barking dog and the talking skeletons made you question whether or not it was real. We're using computer-generated animation to achieve that same reality for today's audiences."

BELOW LEFT TO RIGHT: A Crash McCreery development illustration of a cursed pirate, then ILM and final frame examples of the "reality" conjured up for *The Curse of the Black Pearl*.

Pushing the Envelope

The greatest challenge for *The Curse of the Black Pearl* was how to create the cursed skeleton pirates in such a way that audiences would blink in wonder at how it was all done. Always keenly aware of film history, the movie-loving Verbinski and screenwriters Elliott and Rossio were partially tipping their collective hats to the great Ray Harryhausen, whose stop-motion animation of fantastical creatures, including sword-fighting skeletons in both *The 7th Voyage of Sinbad* and *Jason and the Argonauts* provided so much inspiration for audiences of an earlier generation. "The effect of the pirates turning into living skeletons in the moonlight allowed us to have even more fun with the genre and the characters," says Verbinski. Crash McCreery provided the initial designs for the skeletons, using a Barbossa concept, then all the actors portraying the cursed pirates were photographed in full wardrobe and makeup, followed by visual effects art director Aaron McBride painting each character in a skeletal form. "We went through a couple of revisions until we got approval from Gore on what these characters should look like," says John Knoll.

"From that point," Knoll continues, "we made 3-D body and head scans of the actors. We digitally built one very detailed skeleton that had all the right bones in it. Since everyone's skeleton is a little bit different from everyone else's, the first step was to take the generic skeleton and fit it properly inside the particular person's envelope, or 3-D scan. There was a lot of scaling and smushing to get it to fit."

Following this, a few layers were built to give them what Aaron McBride calls "the dried and desiccated meat look." For that texture, the team scanned in turkey jerky. It was important for the audience to distinguish which skeleton belonged to which character, Knoll points out, so "some of them have particular bits of wardrobe or particular facial features that we carried through. For example, Ragetti has a wooden eye, and he's skinny with bags under his eyes. Pintel has long hair with a bald spot on top, so he's got a lot of exposed skull. Twigg has a beard and a knit cap with a big hole exposing skull through it. And Captain Jack, of course, has his very distinctive dreadlocks."

"When you see the characters as skeletons, you know immediately

ABOVE: Captain Jack Sparrow discovers that he's also under the curse of the Aztec gold; ABOVE RIGHT: Visual development of the skeletal Barbossa by Aaron McBride; RIGHT: An ILM study of the now-cursed Jack Sparrow.

which pirate is which," adds Verbinski, "not just from the actor's voice, but from every nuance, which is why we shot entire scenes only as reference."

Verbinski and director of photography Dariusz Wolski were challenged to find the right way to shoot the fight sequences between the skeletons and the British Navy. "It was equally demanding for George Marshall Ruge, our stunt coordinator, his stunt team, and ultimately for our cameramen," notes Verbinski. "They had to do a lot of handheld composition during the swordplay. First we'd photograph the British sailors and the pirates fighting. Then, we'd do a reference pass with only the sailors, followed by another with only the pirates. We'd be photographing air, and then pan over to a skeleton that wasn't there, saying his line of dialogue, and panning back to another skeleton. We had a lot of technical discussions about how to pull focus to a fictional point of reference while still keeping the excitement of a combat scene. We really didn't want to get into motion control and that sort of static, sterile composition."

ABOVE: In hot pursuit of the *Black Pearl*, the *Flying Dutchman* blasts away with the full force of her cannons; ABOVE RIGHT: Orlando Bloom, Tom Hollander, and Bill Nighy in his gray motion-capture suit; BELOW: Gore Verbinski directs *Flying Dutchman* crewmen in their motion-capture suits on the sands of White Cay in The Exumas.

The Guys in the Little Grey Suits

Dead Man's Chest and *At World's End* each required three times as many visual effects shots as *The Curse of the Black Pearl* did, each film with an increasingly brief and challenging post-production schedule. "The time constraints ILM had to work under were unspeakable," notes Jerry Bruckheimer, "and it's amazing to see the detail and care that's been taken."

"The second and third films are not just a rehash of the first one," says John Knoll. "Gore and the writers came up with a lot of really great and fresh ideas." Knoll sought to free Verbinski up as much as possible to shoot as he wanted without worrying about the visual effects that would come later.

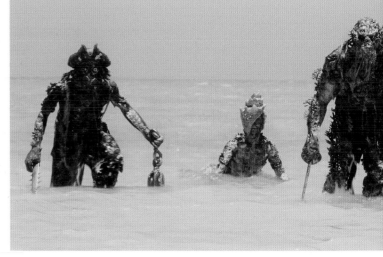

Screenwriters Ted Elliott and Terry Rossio originally conceived of Davy Jones and his crew as ghostlike creatures. Determined to come up with never-before-seen fantastical characters, Verbinski wanted them to be more specifically of the sea, with gravity and weight, as if the souls of shipwrecked sailors had fused with the detritus of the ocean floor. Verbinski turned to his long time collaborators, conceptual consultant Jim Byrkit and creature conceptualist Mark "Crash" McCreery. The remarkably detailed physical manifestations of Jones and his crew were painstakingly worked out by the trio in late night "spitball sessions" fueled by an excess of both caffeine and pure imagination. Audiences and critics alike agreed that Verbinski, Byrkit, and McCreery truly outdid themselves on conceptualizing Jones and his crew, setting ILM to an almost impossible task: make them come to life in all their richness and detail. And although it was always intended for Jones and his sailors to be digitally enhanced, "it was important to have good actors playing those roles," notes Knoll. "A really good actor brings soul to the whole process, and it helps everybody on the set. Gore works with the actor in a very normal way, as he does every other part of the picture. Bill Nighy and all of the actors playing Davy's crew really own the roles. They've thought the characters through, and they're bringing everything they can to these CG characters."

Explains visual effects supervisor Bill George, "We tried something new and challenging on this project. In the past, when you've done a CG character—especially one that's supposed to move like a human—you shoot a clean plate that the character will go into, and at a later time on a different stage you shoot what's called motion capture. This is a process in which you've got a number of cameras, perhaps twelve or fifteen, all focused on a character who's wearing a skintight black suit with little markers on it. Then, as that character moves, using the cameras, the computer triangulates where each point is in space, and therefore the movement. You can then take that animation file and plug it into a character, so that it will move as the actor did onstage. It's a very long and laborious process."

Because of Verbinski's insistence that fantasy look every bit as real as reality, ILM developed new technologies for *Dead Man's Chest* and *At World's End.* "The technology has evolved to the point now," continues George, "where we're trying to capture that exact same data by only using two video cameras as we're shooting the actual shot. The difference now is that instead of splitting it into two separate shoots, it's happening all at the same time. There are a lot of advantages to that. In the first

ABOVE: Filming Keira Knightley as Elizabeth Swann in a tight spot with the *Flying Dutchman* sailors, all wearing their pre-CGI transformation motion-capture suits;
LEFT: In the final version from Industrial Light & Magic, the weird *Dutchman* crew rises from the sea in *Isla Cruces.*

Pirates film, when an actor was fighting one of the cursed skeleton pirates, he was basically fighting with thin air, pretending that someone was there. Now the actors are actually interacting with a real person, which is much more realistic and natural."

"The impact of this is really profound," adds Charlie Gibson, "because so much of the character animation is about nuance of performance, particularly Bill Nighy's. The film is edited based on very subtle facial expressions, attitudes, and even the less tangible things, such as his mood and the feeling behind his eyes, things that you get from a great actor. Bill is a fountainhead of amazing variety. He never repeats himself; there's always some interesting aspect to his performance."

Nighy himself was highly amused by the process in which ILM converted him into the fully tricked-out Davy Jones. "The first thing they did was cyber-scan me, which they did in a sort of mystery truck lined with screens and computers. Then, on set, I wore a gray suit that had reference points comprised of white bubbles and strips of black-and-white material, so that when they come to interpret your physical performance, they're better placed to do so. I don't understand any of it, but you will see that I'm currently the world record holder for playing the organ with an imaginary octopus beard."

In addition to creating skeleton pirates, sea monsters, crustacean sailors, and a maelstrom, visual effects were also utilized in Pirates for considerably more practical purposes. Landscapes were enhanced, structures extended (such as the *Black Pearl*'s and *Flying Dutchman*'s sails), and safety cables and wires erased. In another circumstance, an entire scene that was edited out of *The Curse of the Black Pearl* was modified and restored to *Dead Man's Chest*. Realizing that he needed a shot to establish the pirates' hideaway of Tortuga, Gore Verbinski resurrected a brief moment in which Captain Jack and Will Turner are walking through a scene straight out of the original Pirates of the Caribbean attraction, where the town magistrate is being dunked in a well by a gaggle of mischievous buccaneers. Because at that moment in the *Dead Man's Chest* story Will is off serving on the *Flying Dutchman*, Verbinski shot new elements against a blue screen and then Depp and Bloom were digitally removed and newly-filmed pirates walking through the frame were inserted.

No Less Magical . . . Special Physical Effects

Helping to keep things atmospheric throughout the location shoots were special effects coordinators Terry Frazee on *The Curse of the Black Pearl*, Michael Lantieri and Allen Hall on *Dead Man's Chest*, and John Frazier and Hall on *At World's End*. Whether creating steam and smoke rings from Davy Jones's massive musical organ, smashing full-size ships in half, firing off batteries of cannons, designing and building the intricate mechanics for the runaway-mill-wheel sequence, or laying down massive amounts of smoke and fog around the *Black Pearl* and the *Flying Dutchman*, these physical "in-camera" effects were sometimes almost as magical as ILM's conjurings. So much fog was required for water sequences shot in The Bahamas that Hall had two boats equipped with large jet-pulse engines, not to mention an actual aircraft jet engine mounted on a larger craft. "We actually bought out the world's supply of fog fluid for this movie," Hall confesses.

For *At World's End*, John Frazier—who, in an earlier venture with Jerry Bruckheimer, assisted in the destruction of Pearl Harbor—designed the extraordinarily complex system of motion bases in Palmdale's "Site 9" hangar for the climactic Maelstrom sequence in which the *Black Pearl* and the *Flying Dutchman* engage in final combat while a whirlpool opens up beneath them and darkening clouds swirl overhead. In addition, Frazier also constructed "tilt rigs" on which the *Black Pearl* and *Hai Peng* were capable of leaning to ninety degree angles for the scenes in which the latter vessel goes over the edge of the world—literally—and the former re-emerges into the "real" world in the "Green Flash" sequence.

Crab Balls

Of all the bizarre sights that the Pirates company was privy to, perhaps one of the strangest was the dumping of thousands of lightweight, blue plastic balls onto the deck of the *Black Pearl*. The truth is, they only looked like blue balls, but were, in fact, skittering crabs. Or at least, they would be by the time John Knoll and ILM were finished.

"During the Maelstrom sequence," explains Knoll, "crabs rain over the whole deck of the *Pearl* and sweep away everybody in their path like some kind of crustacean avalanche. Gore came up with the idea of using the balls, like those used in ball pits for children's amusement. He thought they would literally knock everybody off their feet without doing any real damage because of their light weight.

"I might have been inclined to try and accomplish that effect with digital doubles," Knoll continues, "but Gore is a strong proponent of getting as much into the camera as you can and of using visual effects where you really need them. The crabs themselves are computer generated." When the balls rained down upon the company, crew members merrily began to pitch them at each other in all directions . . . including an enthusiastic John Knoll (above right, holding flash),

Locations
PLEASE DO NOT FEED THE IGUANAS

On rough waters off the northeastern coast of Dominica, Gore Verbinski and company were traversing the sea, scouting locations that were inaccessible by land, for *Dead Man's Chest* and *At World's End.* The boat, containing Gore, key production personnel, and an executive from the Walt Disney Studios, joined in the rhythm of the swells, which was getting rougher by the second. Everyone knows that a boat captain's stomach is made of cast iron, but the Dominican helmsman was having trouble keeping his lunch down, and as the swells worsened, he suddenly lunged for the window of the wheelhouse, vomiting copiously and, as (bad) luck would have it, directly on the Disney executive.

Despite this mishap, Verbinski spotted something special. Unable to make a proper landing at the site—especially with the boat's captain still a vivid shade of green—he leaped overboard followed by his team, swam to shore, hauled himself onto the shoals, climbed a steep hill, and discovered the perfect location for a ruined church that would become one of the sites of the phenomenal three-way sword fight between Captain Jack Sparrow, Will Turner, and James Norrington in *Dead Man's Chest.*

This is location scouting, Verbinski style. "We tried to talk Gore out of it," admits Caribbean production supervisor Tom Hayslip, "but he said that if it was easy, we wouldn't be shooting there." Adds executive producer Bruce Hendricks, "If Gore found a location that was inaccessible, that was usually his favorite one."

When Gore Verbinski, Jerry Bruckheimer, and the key production team considered where to find their Caribbean for *The Curse of the Black Pearl,* they decided that although some of it could indeed be artfully re-created on a studio backlot and inside of soundstages, there was really only one direction to go from the safe confines of Los Angeles: southeast—*way* southeast—to the fabled West Indies themselves. "The movie, after all, is called Pirates of the Caribbean, so you don't want to shoot the entire film in Long Beach," says Bruckheimer. "For *The Curse of the Black Pearl,* we found an island untouched by the big developers, very much the way it was many years ago, with a wonderful pristine cove."

OPPOSITE: The three-way sword fight being filmed in production designer Rick Heinrichs's ruined church set in Vielle Casse, Dominica; ABOVE: Verbinski (in hat) and crew prepare to drop coffins off a cliff in Peruvian Vale, St. Vincent, for an opening sequence of *Dead Man's Chest.*

Both land and sea sequences for *The Curse of the Black Pearl* were shot in St. Vincent and the Grenadines, primarily in Wallilabou Bay—where Port Royal and pieces of Tortuga had been designed by Brian Morris—as well as Ottley Hall, the treasure cave entrance in Byhaut, and Petit Tabac ("Little Tobacco"), an outer island in the Grenadines, for the scene in which Captain Jack Sparrow and Elizabeth Swann find themselves stranded by Captain Barbossa on a classic desert island. The St. Vincent and the Grenadines sets for *The Curse of the Black Pearl* were spread over thirty-six miles of open sea, so the marine department, under coordinator Matthew O'Connor had to handle boats for filming and for the transport of some 400 people from land to sea every day.

If the filming of *The Curse of the Black Pearl* was epic, then the simultaneous shooting of *Dead Man's Chest* and *At World's End* could only be described, in the ancient sense, as an odyssey. "It was like fighting a war," recalls *Dead Man's Chest* and *At World's End* executive producer Eric McLeod. "It was a moving army. We had to build roads into places where people never filmed before, up mountainsides, through jungles, down into beaches. The focus is what's happening in front of the camera, but there's a massive circle of support required to get to that place."

In addition to St. Vincent's, Dominica, a green and unspoiled paradise of burgeoning eco-tourism that's just twenty-nine miles long and sixteen miles wide with a population of only 71,000, would serve as the backdrop for an extraordinary range of locations. "We selected Dominica as a major location because it's beautiful and virtually untouched," notes Bruckheimer. "Because it has such a jagged coastline, they can't get cruise ships in, which prevents the island from becoming overly developed. You're not seeing the same landscapes, jungles, and mountains as you have in other movies. Dominica is a gorgeous island, but some of the amenities aren't there. We employed a lot of people on the island, and they were brilliant and wonderful to work with. But if a piece of equipment breaks down, it takes at least two days to get it replaced from off-island, so we had daunting production challenges. The hotels weren't exactly fancy, but everybody bonded together. It was like going to camp. A lot of the cast and crew lived in cabins, slept under mosquito netting, and had dinners on the beach. We really had to make do."

BELOW LEFT and RIGHT: Underwater photographers shoot on *The Curse of the Black Pearl.*

"Dominica is what the Caribbean looked like 200 years ago," notes Bruce Hendricks. "You need the wildness and natural beauty that some of the more offbeat and remote places, like Dominica, offer. Gore, like any great director, pushes you to go a step beyond. The great ones have to be leading the charge

up the hill, they have to be the ones with the vision to push frontiers and boundaries, both artistically and technically. A rational person would not go there, and they wouldn't take along 500 of their closest friends and hundreds of tons of equipment. It takes purpose and single-mindedness to pull off something like that, and Gore is all of that, and more."

Dominica would present massive challenges for Rick Heinrichs and construction coordinator Greg Callas. "Because supplies are so limited on Dominica, we had to bring in our own hardware store: every nail, piece of wood, sack of cement and plaster, and gallon of paint. The equipment we take for granted, like scissor lifts, boom lifts, and forklifts, don't exist in Dominica, so we imported them from other countries in the Caribbean and South America. We implemented a lot of old-school construction, because we didn't have the luxury of the twenty-first century there."

The Indian River, a gorgeous stretch of shallow water flowing into the ocean at Portsmouth in the northeast of Dominica, portrayed the Pantano River in *Dead Man's Chest*. Because of the river's ecological sensitivity, cast, crew, and equipment had to be sent upriver in boats that were either manually rowed or utilized electric motors only (no outboards). For anyone heading back upriver at dark after wrap, the massive fireflies doing figure-eights in the night sky were also reminders of the ride. (However, the fireflies seen flitting along the Pantano River in *Dead Man's Chest* were added in post-production by Industrial Light & Magic.)

During production, the crew became not unlike pirates themselves, albeit of a kinder, gentler nature. The Jolly Roger was proudly flown from many a production vehicle and support craft, several crew members sprouted tattoos, some pierced their ears or noses, or wore head scarves or bandanas, and some wore silver or gold skull-and-crossbones rings especially designed by makeup artist Joel Harlow. Many wore T-shirts displaying the words "Livin' the Ride"—and a wild ride it was.

In The Exumas, the spit of almost pink, fine sand called White Cay served as the location for the three-way sword fight in *Dead Man's Chest* as well as the Parlay sequence in *At World's End*. White Cay was only accessible by water, so

the company was required to drive southeast from the hotel zone and board one of many boats which brought them to a floating base camp comprised of two 200-foot barges tethered together, on which one could find an entire floating base of operations—actors' trailers, equipment trucks, catering tent, tables, and chairs. From there, it took another boat ride before making a wet beach landing on the cay. Verbinski required 360-degree angles, hence the necessity of keeping the cay clear of trucks, vehicles, and equipment. The company could only shoot in specific tidal conditions, which limited the number of hours available for filming.

"Please do not feed the iguanas," implored the call sheets while shooting on White Cay, so as to protect the friendly, indigenous lizard population from the affectionate attentions of the company.

Work commenced on the fourth and final location, The Bahamas Film Studio at Gold Rock Creek on Grand Bahama Island, in fall 2005. Late September was theoretically the tail end of storm season. Following an initial week of literal smooth sailing in beautiful weather, Mother Nature threw her first knuckleball at the *Dead Man's Chest* company, drenching the island in buckets of torrential rain and stirring up the seas to an angry froth. "When you're working on water," explains Jerry Bruckheimer, "the weather changes constantly, the wind shifts, and the waves go in different directions, which makes it difficult to work. We're very conscious of safety, and we had our marine unit move the vessels, shepherd us back and forth from land to sea, get food out to cast and crew working on the ships, and take them back to shore at night. Along with our marine unit, we also had expert divers."

"It's true what they say about water," said Gore Verbinski. "Everything that can go wrong will go wrong, that's just the way it works. As soon as you get a boat in position, the wind changes. Even if you anchor things down,

"It's been amazing at every level, you become kind of like a weird gypsy family, a traveling circus."

—JOHNNY DEPP

everything is moving, relationships are moving. The camera is here and we frame a shot of the actor, then everything is drifting away. Or, the wind is right to fill the sails, but then the sun is in the wrong direction, and if you want a good backlight, then the sails are negative." But Verbinski was never one to just throw up his hands in frustration and give up. "Come on, let's make lemonade out of lemons," was his eternally optimistic order of the day.

When the company went to sleep on Grand Bahama Island on the night of October 18, 2005, Wilma was only a category-one hurricane somewhere south of Cuba—still quite a distance, but close enough for discomfort. By the next morning, it had graduated not only to a category five, but also to new status as the most powerful hurricane in recorded history. The decision was made by all involved to immediately evacuate the company, with three chartered jets flying them out on October 19. "Fortunately for us," recalls Bruckheimer. "we got everybody out, locked down our ships in the harbor, and had them all battened down. We had only minor damage considering what could have happened."

About forty Pirates crew members stayed behind on Grand Bahama during the hurricane. Some, like Caribbean production supervisor Tom Hayslip and much of Dan Malone's marine department, ensured the safety of the ships. Others, like behind-the-scenes videographer Jack Kney, chronicled the event, and fortunately all got through safely. Elliott and Rossio subsequently added a hurricane reference in an exchange of dialogue on the deck of the *Black Pearl* near the opening scenes of *Dead Man's Chest*.

Two days before the company wrapped on Grand Bahama, the location filming came full circle during the climactic sequence for *At World's End* in which the pirates of the *Black Pearl* unfurl the Jolly Roger and raise it high over the masts. As a speaker blared Hans Zimmer's huge, stirring music written expressly for this scene, goosebumps started to appear on the arms of virtually the entire company. Pirates, living the film for real.

The final three days of the 284-day-long combined shoot of *Dead Man's Chest* and *At World's End*, from January 8 to 10, 2007 (nearly two years after the cameras first rolled), saw two of the world's most beautiful islands "standing in" for the Caribbean. A reduced company traveled from Los Angeles to Hawaii, where they filmed key scenes with Orlando Bloom and Keira Knightley on a sweeping, dramatic cliffside in Maui, and then a magnificent beach dotted with black volcanic rocks on Molokai.

The latter island, with its staggering 1,700-foot sea cliffs, has a population of 7,500 souls, known for their kindness and aloha (this is where Father Damien tended to those afflicted with Hansen's disease in the late nineteenth century at the still-extant colony at Kalaupapa). And that hospitality was never so well demonstrated as at the real down-home luau celebration for Jerry Bruckheimer and company after Gore Verbinski called the final "cut" on the beach at sunset. With a pig roasting in the underground imu oven, tasty mai tais, live island music, and a lovely local hula troupe, the epic shoot ended on as high a note as any of the weather-beaten crew could have hoped for.

Pirates By the Numbers
Compiled by executive producer Eric McLeod

6 countries

141 Second Unit filming days

178 barrels of smoke used by special effects

256 ³/8 script pages

281 First Unit filming days

475 cell phones distributed in Dominica

550 barrels built by set dressing

3,490 hours, **24** minutes of filming

4,000+ crew members

6,000+ batteries used by the sound department

463,000 feet of rope rigged or used

10,000 one-way tickets to locations, not including charter flights

2,862,690 feet (**471** nautical miles) of film

AFTERWORD
Bring Me That Horizon

November 2006: Palmdale, California. Late afternoon Friday, November 17, 2006. The 256th day of the combined *Dead Man's Chest* and *At World's End* shoot. For all of that day and the one preceding, the usual raucous and explosively noisy atmosphere of filming inside the Site 9 hangar has given way to a hushed, almost cathedral-like mood. In front of an oversized green screen is the strange sight of a gigantic version of Captain Jack Sparrow's dreadlocks. Mischievously peeking out from the oversized beads that dangle from the matted hair is Johnny Depp as the good captain in a surreally comic scene for *At World's End,* which also happens to be his very last required piece of acting. Only Depp is working this day—the hundreds of extras and stunt players who usually populate the set are taking a day of rest. The company, while thoroughly exhausted by the long-distance duration of the shoot, is still somehow holding it together, still on their toes, still giving everything they have to the production.

On both days, members of the crew seem almost confused as the realization dawns that Depp's departure is imminent—proof that filming is, incredibly, drawing to a finale. "It's not a gig, it's a lifestyle," is a refrain often heard amidst the company—you wake up, you get dressed, you go pirating for twelve to fourteen hours a day, and you keep doing it week after week, month after month, and, for that matter, year after year. The previous week has seen bittersweet good-byes to the other stars: first Keira Knightley, followed by Geoffrey Rush, then Orlando Bloom.

Although Depp completes his last scene at about noon, he's put in a holding pattern until Gore Verbinski learns whether or not some footage shot the day before has made it cleanly from the camera to processing in the lab. Six hours later, the word comes in that all looks fine, which means that Johnny Depp is free to leave.

Except it's four years, one month, and eight days after *The Curse of the Black Pearl* first commenced filming, and Depp isn't quite sure that he wants to.

"The possibility of saying good-bye to Captain Jack perhaps forever is not one I look forward to," he said about a month earlier while filming in the Rancho Guadalupe Dunes near Santa Maria, California. "But if that is the case, we had a good run. I know Captain Jack will always make me smile. Pirates has done a lot for me, and in every way you can imagine. But most importantly, what I've felt is this intense, pure joy. Playing this character and being this character and delivering this character will always bring a smile to my face, always make me happy and proud."

In the hangar, a large pastry that looks for all the world like a birthday cake for a little boy who's crazy about pirates, replete with toy figures and little ships, is positioned next to the shooting set. Images of Captain Jack made of edible buttercream surround the words:

DEAREST
CAPTAIN JACK
MAY YOUR COMPASS ALWAYS
LEAD YOU BACK TO US
THANK YOU

Suddenly, all work comes to a quick halt as Depp enters the area for the farewell ceremony. "So it's Johnny's last day on the movie," says Gore Verbinski to the assembled crew members, "the man who's employed us all over these last four years. I want to say 'thank you.' It's been fun to know you, a friend, ally, and partner in this madness. Let's hear it for Captain Jack!"

The group explodes into cheers and applause, and Depp, now out of costume, looks shy, humble, and deeply moved. "I'll be incredibly brief," he says, "because I may weep. You guys have made this the most amazing experience of my life, except for having my kids. I'd go to war with any of you.

"I'm going to call this a break, or a hiatus, or something . . . it's happened to us before, hasn't it? But I don't feel like I can say good-bye. Certainly not to any of you . . . and not to Captain Jack, either. Thank you for the ride."

The champagne, tears, laughter, and fellowship that follows lasts quite a bit of time before the company buckles back down to work to complete a long night of shooting. There are several hours more to film, and another ten days or so of principal photography until Verbinski calls the final wrap.

And although the future is a great and wide mystery, we can only hope that, as Johnny Depp said, there really are no good-byes to be said.

OPPOSITE: The last photo taken of Johnny Depp as Captain Jack Sparrow on his final day of filming *At World's End.*

Acknowledgments

There are approximately a thousand people sprinkled across the seven seas and the several continents who deserve to be profusely thanked and profoundly acknowledged, most of whom are the entire, unbelievably dedicated cast and crew of the Pirates of the Caribbean movies. This book is merely the sum total of their brilliant creativity and hard work. The Pirates company were my companions, my friends, and my extended family for nearly two years of the fabulous adventure that was the filming of *Dead Man's Chest* and *At World's End*. Very special thanks to Jerry Bruckheimer, the admiral, for allowing me to take an extraordinary journey that changed my life; to Gore Verbinski, the captain, for his encouragement and inspiration; and to our production chiefs Mike Stenson, Chad Oman, Bruce Hendricks, Eric McLeod, and Doug Merrifield; appreciation to everyone at the Walt Disney Studios and Jerry Bruckheimer Films, especially Dennis Rice, Charlie Nelson, Ryan Stankevich, Dora Candelaria, Christine Cadena, and Jon Rogers at the former, and KristieAnne Reed and Diane Drummond at the latter. I salute Jody Revenson of Disney Editions, an editor who praised and pushed at all the right moments, the best any writer could hope for; a multitude of thanks to Gabriela Gutentag, who as unit publicist of *The Curse of the Black Pearl* provided me with a firm foundation of material on which to build the rest, and whose encouragement has always meant the world to me; gratitude to Jack Kney, Mark Herzog, Mark Cowen, and the great staff at Herzog-Cowen Entertainment; to Jason Surrell for his superb book *Pirates of the Caribbean: From the Magic Kingdom to the Movies*, a splendid prequel to the tale told in this volume; and to the brilliant Imagineers past and present who created, maintained, and then enhanced the original attraction at the Disney theme parks.

The dedication for this book is simpler to accomplish. This is for my wife, Yuko, and our daughters, Miyako and Kimiko—for their endless love, patience, and support while I spent months away from home, whether in the Caribbean or Palmdale.

Domo arigato gozaimasu, my loves.

—Michael Singer

The book's producers would like to thank the following for their contributions to this book: Steve Borell, John Bernstein, Michael Buckhoff, Holly Clark, Guy Cunningham, Morgan Feeney, Jonathan Heely, Brian Hoffman, Gary Kleinman, Sharon Krinsky, Kevin Monroe, Tracey Ramos, David Rominger, Erik Schmudde, Dave Smith, Kim Snyder, Muriel Tebid, Robert Tieman, and MaryBeth Tregarthen.

Additionally, we'd like to express our deep gratitude to Christine Cadena and Jon Rogers.